Table of Contents

Recipes have been tested in U.S. Standard measurements. Common metric measurements are given as a convenience for those who are more familiar with metric. Recipes have not been tested in metric.

Dymond Lake Seasoning (DLS) is used in many of our recipes. It is our own unique blend of herbs and spices. It contains no MSG. If you are unable to find DLS, seasoned salt and/or seasoned pepper may be substituted. For each recipe that uses DLS, we have suggested appropriate alternatives. These vary from recipe to recipe to try to approximate the special flavors that DLS emphasizes in each recipe. To order Dymond Lake Seasoning, see page 207.

Introduction

TO YOU OUR GUESTS

Hunting, fishing and cooking are all skills that are avidly pursued by enthusiasts, each according to his or her own persuasion. Hunting and fishing are rewarding in their own right, and even more so when the trophy lake trout or the elusive Ross's Goose or the gigantic caribou antlers can be proudly displayed at the end of a trip, but surely the "icing on the cake" is the sampling of the day's catch!

The collection of recipes in this book is the result of endless requests from guests both at North Knife Lake Fishing Lodge and Dymond Lake Hunting Lodge, where the preparation of the meals is an art in itself. The tantalizing variety of fresh fish shore lunches cooked up by the guides, the expert preparation of fresh geese and native berries, the freshly baked bread and buns that accompany every meal, the agonizingly irresistible desserts to round off the feast — all are collected here so that the pleasure need not end when you leave the camps.

What about the title of our book? This whole endeavor, the camps, the cooking, the friendship, grew out of Churchill, the Polar Bear Capital of the World. One of the challenges has been and will still be to find new ways to prepare the natural produce of our northern habitat. Besides that, what do you think the cooks are doing while you are out hunting and fishing? When the season is right, they're out picking blueberries!

This is our offering to you, with love

Helen Webber
Marie Woolsey

TO YOU OUR ENTHUSIASTS

We have not written this cookbook only for the pleasure of those who have experienced the camps. Good cooking is to be appreciated by all who desire it. Many of the recipes can be adapted to use your own local berries and meats, and we encourage you to experiment, as we have. Nor are the recipes restricted to "game food". They encompass all that we cook and serve, and you can be sure that they have been well tested by some of the world's best critics — those who have paid for the privilege. If they think we should write them all down, who are we to argue?

This, then, is our offering to you, as well, with love

Helen Webber
Marie Woolsey

From Helen and Marie

You could say that *Blueberries and Polar Bears* is primarily a cookbook but we have written it to be more than that. We have included short stories and notes to give you a glimpse of what life has been like for one young wife plucked out of Southern Ontario and dropped in the middle of a northern native village (Marie); and another (Helen) who grew up in Churchill, Manitoba, a very isolated community. She thought that was as rugged as it was going to get but Doug had even more isolation in mind — the fly-in lodges. So in this book we have combined the recipes we use at the lodges with some of the predicaments in which we have found ourselves. I feel the book reflects the pioneer spirit that both Marie and I have. We have gone into unknown territory and risen to the challenges that have come our way.

The impetus for writing *Blueberries and Polar Bears* came from the guests themselves. For 25 years, Helen has been entertaining and cooking for guests, first at Dymond Lake Lodge, and then at North Knife Lake Lodge, both in Northern Manitoba. Marie has been helping out for many of those years. The guests have convinced us that the food we serve is above average and deserves to be shared. Thousands of satisfied guests can't be wrong! This book will fill the need for those who want to take a bit of the north home with them. But we are hoping that it will appeal to many others who have a love of the wilderness and an adventuresome spirit. It is written with humor and reveals much of our personalities because we know, personally, many of the people for whom we are writing.

As the idea began to gel, we decided that we wanted an even broader appeal. So, although the focal point may seem to be wild meat, that is only one section of the book. *Blueberries and Polar Bears* actually contains recipes for every part of the day, from breakfast through evening snacks; and for every occasion, whether camping out, cooking for your family or entertaining special guests. The collection of recipes in this book is practical cooking and baking recipes that any new cook would appreciate. Nothing is terribly difficult, since preparation time is of the essence at the camps. In our years of cooking together, Helen and I have done much experimenting — we are not above trying out new recipes on our guests. They are the best critics in the world. We only reuse the recipes that get rave reviews — ho-hum is never good enough. But our book also contains delicious traditional recipes such as stuffed turkey and prime rib. It is difficult to focus on any one area that gets more raves than another — but after the breads, which are unanimously acclaimed, and goose and fish dishes, our desserts would be a close fourth. No meal is complete until the Final Temptation has been offered (and they are rarely rejected).

Our hope is that *Blueberries and Polar Bears*, itself, will be a temptation that is too difficult to refuse.

Introduction   5

She "Don't" Do Mornings

(HELEN) Breakfast starts early at the lodges. At North Knife, our fishing lodge, we have the first breakfast on the table at 6:30 a.m. for the guides, and the guests start to arrive at 7:00 a.m. At Dymond Lake, our hunting lodge, the first breakfast is at 4:30 a.m. for the guides and at 5:00 a.m. for the guests. It is hard to get too enthusiastic at 4:00 a.m. but somehow we manage. You can't believe how much work you can get done by noon if your day starts at 4 a.m. That does remind me of a cute story!

Back in the dawn of time, when we had just built our first two cabins at Dymond Lake, my sister, Maureen, came over to help me out for the three weeks. Now this was back in the days before we had any running water or refrigerators or electricity or anything that resembled a modern convenience. We had to heat all our water for dishes, mix all our bread and baking by hand and just generally work from 4:00 a.m. to at least 11:00 p.m. almost nonstop. (Now with all our modern conveniences we make it to bed by 9:30 or 10:00 p.m. and sometimes even have time for some berry picking or occasionally a nap in the afternoon.) Maureen is one great person but she doesn't really like mornings to begin with so you can imagine that after a couple of weeks of this schedule her mornings and nights were getting a little confused.

Anyway, one evening our work was going on a bit longer than usual. It was getting on to 11:30 p.m. and we were still in the kitchen. I knew the bacon was still slightly frozen and decided it would make our morning go a little easier if we brought it in (the icebox was outside) and left it on the counter to thaw. I just casually looked at Maureen and asked "Will you go out and get the bacon?" She looked at me with a look of pure disbelief and asked "Have I slept already?"

Dymond Lake Prayer

For Honkers young and Honkers old
For Honkers hot and Honkers cold
For Honkers tender, Honkers tough
We thank Thee, Lord, we've had enough.

Moose, Goose
&
Things That Swim

Marie coined this phrase for our wild game section and we all loved it. I was born and raised in Churchill. When Doug came to town — looking very dashing in his Royal Canadian Navy uniform, I married him thinking he would take me off to see "The World". Surprise, Surprise, he fell in love with Churchill as well as me and when the Navy left — we stayed! He quickly became involved in the hunting and fishing in the area. Marie was raised in southern Ontario but very soon after marrying Gary, who was a Priest/Pilot for the Anglican Church, she found herself living in small, remote native villages in northern Ontario and Manitoba. In both of these settings, we found ourselves faced with a lot of wild game and fish which we had to learn to cook and appreciate. Sometimes there was nothing else in the freezer. It was a challenge which we both enjoyed. What you find here are the tastier results of our experiences! We are not finished; we are always looking for new, exciting recipes for moose, goose and things that swim!

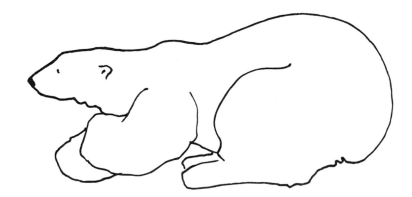

Wild Meatball Taste Teasers

Helen's daughter, Shari, is a natural cook (which she comes by naturally), who naturally loves to experiment. This is her invention and it is delectable — naturally!

2 lbs.	ground caribou (moose, deer OR elk)	1 kg
3 tbsp.	soy sauce	45 mL
1 tbsp.	brown sugar	15 mL
10 oz.	can water chestnuts, finely chopped	284 mL
½ cup	finely chopped onion	125 mL
1 tsp.	dried parsley flakes OR 1 tbsp. (15 mL) chopped fresh parsley	5 mL
2	garlic cloves, minced OR ½ tsp. (2 mL) garlic powder	2 mL

1. Mix all ingredients together in a large bowl.
2. Shape into bite-sized balls (approximately 4 dozen).
3. Place meatballs on a greased baking sheet with sides and bake in a 375°F (190°C) oven for 15 minutes.

Makes about 4 dozen meatballs.

SERVING SUGGESTIONS: Serve hot with the following fruit sauce or sauce of your choice. Center fruit sauce on a glass plate and surround with meatballs. Provide picks. Now enjoy!

NOTE: If you make these ahead, just reheat them in the oven at 400°F (200°C) for 5 minutes.

See photograph on page 103.

Fruit Sauce

3 tbsp.	cider vinegar	45 mL
1 cup	apricot OR peach jam	250 mL
¼ tsp.	paprika	1 mL

1. Combine all ingredients and pour into a small glass dish.

See photograph on page 103.

Gavin's Caribou Strips

Gavin is Helen's brother-in-law. We have watched a strange phenomenon develop through the years. We used to exchange recipes with sisters and sisters-in-law but nowadays it is just as likely to be one of the males in the family who has just found or produced a great recipe. This hors d'oeuvre is a winner. We have even served it to the Lieutenant Governor of Manitoba.

2 lbs.	caribou strips, approximately ½ by 2½" (1 x 6 cm)	1 kg
1 cup	flour	250 mL
2 tsp.	DLS* OR 1 tsp. (5mL) each of seasoned salt & pepper	10 mL
¼ cup	vegetable oil	60 mL
2 tbsp.	butter OR margarine	30 mL

Garlicky Wine Marinade:

2 cups	dry red wine	500 mL
2	garlic cloves, crushed	2
2 tbsp.	soy sauce	30 mL
½ tsp.	dry mustard	2 mL

1. Combine all of the marinade ingredients and add the caribou strips. Marinate in the refrigerator for 8 hours, or overnight if it is more convenient.
2. Mix the flour and seasoning. Dredge** the drained caribou strips in the flour and sauté*** in the oil and butter, a handful at a time, until nicely browned. You may have to add more oil and butter.
3. Serve with wooden toothpicks.

Makes 8 dozen strips.

SERVING SUGGESTIONS: These taste great alone or you can serve them with a sauce for dipping such as the Fruit Sauce on page 8. Another great-tasting and very simple dipping sauce is ¼ cup (60 mL) of your favorite bottled barbecue sauce mixed with ¼ cup (60 mL) peach or apricot jam!

* *Dymond Lake Seasoning*
** *DREDGE: To shake in flour until completely coated.*
*** *SAUTÉ: To fry quickly, stirring constantly over high heat to seal in the juices.*

See photograph on page 103.

Miner's Steak

We haven't had too many miners at the lodges but all the fishermen and hunters go for this dish in a big way. If you don't have the moose or caribou on hand I am sure it would be just as good with elk or deer. And if you are really desperate you can always try beef. This is an especially easy dish to prepare because it doesn't have to be browned first!

¼ cup	flour	60 mL
1 tsp.	salt	5 mL
¼ tsp.	pepper	1 mL
1 tsp.	DLS* OR use ½ tsp. (2 mL) seasoned pepper	5 mL
1½ lbs.	moose or caribou round steak cut into ½" (1.3 cm) strips	750 g
1	large onion, sliced	1
1	green pepper, sliced	1
10 oz.	can mushrooms, drained	284 mL
1 tbsp.	molasses	15 mL
3 tbsp.	soy sauce	45 mL
1 cup	beef broth	250 mL
19 oz.	can tomatoes, chopped	540 mL

1. Combine the flour, salt, pepper and DLS* in a plastic bag.
2. Shake the meat strips in the flour mixture and place in a Dutch oven or roaster.
3. Place the onions, peppers and mushrooms over the meat.
4. Combine the molasses, soy sauce, beef broth and tomatoes and pour over the meat and vegetables.
5. Cover and bake at 325°F (160°C) for 2½-3 hours. Stir once or twice while baking.

Serves 6

SERVING SUGGESTIONS: This is wonderful served over noodles.

NOTE: This recipe doubles or triples well if you are feeding a crowd.

* Dymond Lake Seasoning

FIRST SPORTSMAN "It's getting awfully late and we haven't hit a thing yet."
SECOND SPORTSMAN "Let's miss two more and then go home."

Moose, Goose & Things That Swim

Moose Pot Roast — 2 Ways!

This makes a dandy hot moose sandwich. Just pile the meat on a nice crusty roll and serve au jus, with bowls of the unthickened natural juices for dipping. Add some baked beans and a tossed salad and you are all set.

4 lbs.	moose OR caribou roast (one of the tougher cuts)	2 kg
1½ oz.	onion soup mix (1 envelope)	40 g
2 x 10 oz.	cans beef consommé	2 x 284 mL
2 x 10 oz.	cans water	2 x 284 mL

1. Place the roast in a roaster and sprinkle with onion soup mix. Add consommé and water.
2. Cover and cook at 275°F (140°C) for 5 hours.
3. Slice roast (if it hasn't fallen apart already), serve on split crusty rolls with the juice from the pan for dipping.

Serves 10-12.

VARIATIONS: I have used the above method on goose pieces also. You can cut the cooking time down to 3½-4 hours.

Instead of serving the roast au jus, I thickened the pan juices with flour and water for a gravy. Very good!

Mushroom Onion Pot Roast

| 1½ oz. | onion soup mix (1 envelope) | 40 g |
| 2 x 10 oz. | cans mushroom soup | 2 x 284 mL |

1. Mix onion soup mix with mushroom soup. Pour over roast in roaster.
2. Put the lid on, put roast in the oven and cook as above. Thin gravy with water, if necessary, before serving.

SERVING SUGGESTION: This version is great with mashed potatoes and a salad. The gravy is already made when you take off the lid!

Moose or Caribou Wellington

This recipe is outstanding. I have served it many times and have always had rave reviews. You can either use frozen puff pastry or, if you want to be a purist, the Puff Pastry recipe on page 186 is really very simple.

2 tbsp.	butter	30 mL
1 tbsp.	oil	15 mL
3 lbs.	tenderloin, (moose OR caribou, cut into 1½" (4 cm) slices for rare, 1" (2.5 cm) slices for medium and ¾" (2 cm) slices for well done salt and pepper OR DLS* to taste	1.5 kg

Mushroom Pâté:

2 tbsp.	butter	30 mL
¼ cup	finely chopped onion	60 mL
¾ lb.	fresh mushrooms, very finely chopped	375 g
1 tsp.	DLS* OR ½ tsp. (2 mL) salt and ¼ tsp. (1 mL) pepper	5 mL
1 tbsp.	dry sherry OR brandy	15 mL
1 lb.	puff pastry, purchased OR homemade	500 g
1	egg yolk	1
1 tbsp.	water	15 mL

1. TO PREPARE THE MEAT, heat the butter and oil in a heavy frying pan over high heat and quickly sear** both sides of the tenderloin slices just until nicely browned, about 1 minute per side. Remove from the pan and set aside to cool.
2. TO MAKE THE MUSHROOM PÂTÉ, melt the butter in a frying pan.
3. Add the onions and cook about 1 minute.
4. Add the mushrooms which should be very finely chopped. (A food processor works best, slice them thickly and just them a quick whir in the processor.)
5. Sprinkle with the DLS* or salt and pepper and continue to cook for about ten minutes, or until all the juices have cooked off.
6. Add the sherry or brandy and transfer to a bowl.
7. Cover and refrigerate until cool.
8. TO PREPARE THE PUFF PASTRY, on a floured surface, roll out the pastry to ⅛" (3 mm) thickness. Cut into 6 squares which should be large enough to completely envelop the meat slices with at least 1" (2.5 cm) overlap for sealing.

Moose or Caribou Wellington

9. HERE'S HOW TO PUT IT ALL TOGETHER, cover both sides of the meat slices with the Mushroom Pâté.
10. Place 1 slice on each square of pastry.
11. Beat the egg yolk with the water and use it to brush the edges of the pastry.
12. Fold the pastry around the meat and seal very well on all edges, folding the edges to the bottom.
13. Place the packages seam side down on a baking sheet that has been sprinkled with flour. Make sure that they don't touch each other.
14. Set in a cool place and let rest for 1 hour before cooking.
15. Brush the pastry with the egg yolk. You can also use any pastry scraps to decorate the top of the packages. Brush the decorations with the egg yolk as well to be sure they brown nicely.
16. Pierce the packages with a fork, in a couple of places to allow the steam to escape. Bake in a preheated oven at 400°F (200°C) for 20 minutes, or until pastry is golden brown.

Serves 6.

* *Dymond Lake Seasoning*

** *SEAR: To brown very quickly with the application of intense heat. It can also mean to burn. Please don't!*

Two hunters had been out for several hours and one of them had been growing uneasy. Finally, panic overtook him.

"We're lost!" he cried to his companion, "What on earth shall we do?"

"Keep your shirt on!" said his unruffled companion. "Shoot an extra deer and the game warden will be here in a minute and a half."

Moose, Goose & Things That Swim   13

Dymond Lake Goose Gumbo

A very special thank you to Helyn at The Ferris in Eagle Lake, Texas for intro-ducing us to this recipe!! When Marie and I decided to try it, neither of us had ever eaten a gumbo. Not to worry though. Gumbo is what we call the thick mud along the mud flats of Hudson Bay, so we thought — okay, this has to have a nice thick consistency. "Not so!" our deep-south guests told us when we added it to our Dymond Lake menu. Apparently, authentic gumbo is like a very thin soup. But they urged us not to change ours one bit, so we haven't and here it is!

	breasts and legs from 8 geese	
2 tbsp.	DLS* OR 2 tsp. (10 mL) seasoned salt and 1 tsp. (5 mL) pepper	30 mL
1 tsp.	cayenne pepper	5 mL
	Louisiana Hot Sauce OR Tabasco, to taste	
¼ cup	bacon drippings, melted	60 mL
2 cups	bacon drippings	500 mL
2 cups	flour	500 mL
2 cups	finely diced celery	500 mL
2 cups	finely diced green pepper	500 mL
2½ cups	finely chopped onion	625 mL
3	garlic cloves, crushed	3
2 qts.	boiling water	2 L
1	bunch green onions, chopped	1

1. Place the breasts and legs in a shallow roasting or baking pan. Sprinkle liberally with the DLS* or seasoned salt and pepper, cayenne and the Hot Sauce or Tabasco. Drizzle about ¼ cup (60 mL) melted bacon drippings over the goose.
2. Place the goose in a 400°F (200°C) oven. Turn the pieces over after 20 minutes to brown the other side. Check after 20 more minutes and, if necessary, pour in a small amount of boiling water so that it will steam. We usually find that there is already enough liquid.
3. Cover and return to the oven at 325°F (160°C) for 2-3 hours, or until the meat is falling off the leg bones.
4. Remove the roaster from the oven and remove the meat from the pan. When it is cool enough to handle cut the meat into bite-sized pieces and set aside. Leave the juice in the pan for the next step.
5. Begin heating the 2 cups (500 mL) of bacon drippings in a heavy pot over medium heat. When the drippings are melted add the flour and stir continuously, using a wire whisk. Do not let the flour stick or burn. Continue stirring and cooking until the roux** is the color of cocoa. You don't want it too pale but too dark gives a slightly burnt flavor.

Moose, Goose & Things That Swim

Dymond Lake Goose Gumbo

Continued

6. When the roux has reached the proper color, add the celery, green pepper, onions and garlic. Be sure you have on an oven mitt   the roux will bubble and steam when you throw in the vegetables. Cook, stirring often, until the vegetables are limp, about 15 minutes.
7. At this point, heat the reserved pan juices to boiling and add them slowly to the roux, stirring continuously to keep it smooth.
8. Next, add 4 cups (1 L) of boiling water, again stirring constantly to keep the roux smooth. Add another 3-4 cups (750 mL-1 L) boiling water to make the gumbo a nice thick stew-like consistency.
9. Add the diced goose. Simmer until all the flavors have blended, at least 45 minutes. Taste and add salt, pepper and cayenne as needed. The flavor should be hot and spicy.

Serves 12 or more

SERVING SUGGESTIONS: *We eat the gumbo spooned over a bowl of rice and topped with chopped green onions.*

NOTE: *Don't be intimidated by the length of this recipe. Once you have done it you will see that it is quite simple and delicious.*

* *Dymond Lake Seasoning*
** *ROUX: A cooked mixture of flour and fat, used as a flavoring and thickening agent in soups, stews and gravies.*

The Selkirk Grace

Some hae meat, and canna eat,
And some wad eat that want it,
But we hae meat and we can eat,
And sae the Lord be thankit.
                    Robbie Burns

Goose Tidbits

(HELEN) This was the first appetizer I learned to make at Dymond Lake, over 20 years ago. The recipe was given to me by one of our hunters. I have found the hunters to be the best source of excellent wild game recipes. We still make goose tidbits for every group that comes to Dymond and they still rave about them. And it is such a simple recipe. This is best done with YVGB (Doug's abbreviation for young, virgin, goose boobies).

> **several goose breasts**
> **butter — the real thing!**
> **DLS* OR seasoned pepper**
> **white vermouth**

1. Lay the goose breast flat on the cutting board and, with a sharp knife, slice along the top to make very thin slices.
2. Melt 2 tbsp. (30 mL) butter in a heavy frying pan over medium-high heat until it is sizzling.
3. Lay the goose slices in the frying pan and sprinkle liberally with DLS* or seasoned pepper. They should brown quite quickly. If they do not, turn up the heat a bit. When they are nicely browned on one side turn them over, sprinkle liberally again with DLS* or seasoned pepper. Brown for about a minute.
4. Splash in about ¼ cup (60 mL) of white vermouth. Let the breasts simmer in the vermouth for about a minute.
5. Remove from pan and serve immediately, with toothpicks.
6. Repeat the process until you have enough appetizers.

* *Dymond Lake Seasoning*

See photograph on page 103.

Wild Goose

Jalapeño Goose Breasts Suprême, page 20
Marie's Wild Rice Casserole Suprême, page 126
Broccoli Salad, page 115
Onion Salad, page 123

Duck Taste Teaser With Bacon & Water Chestnuts

A very long name for a very simple but yummy recipe!

1 cup	dry red wine	250 mL
2	garlic cloves, minced, OR ½ tsp. (2 mL) garlic powder	2
1 tbsp.	soy sauce	15 mL
6-8	duck breasts OR 3-4 young goose breasts, cut into bite-sized pieces	6-8
10 oz.	can sliced water chestnuts	284 mL
1 lb.	thinly sliced bacon strips, halved	454 g

1. Combine red wine, garlic and soy sauce in a large bowl. Add the duck pieces and marinate in the refrigerator for 24 hours.
2. Remove duck pieces from the marinade, place a slice of water chestnut on each side, wrap with a bacon strip and secure with a wooden pick. They may be prepared ahead to this point, covered and refrigerated.
3. Roast at 350°F (180°C) for 25-30 minutes, until bacon is cooked. Serve hot!

Makes 3 dozen.

See photograph on page 103.

Cards, Anyone?

The year my sister, Maureen, helped at Dymond Lake, we had a few bears hanging around. Now Maureen is like the rest of us, she loves polar bears but she prefers THEM to be where SHE isn't. One morning when she was walking from one cabin to the other to do the cleaning, she caught sight of a bear on the other side of the cabin. This tends to speed up the heartbeat considerably. After the bear went on its way, she came back to the main cabin and nonchalantly took a deck of cards and a flashlight and set them on the corner of one of the tables. Then she took a chair and set it next to the trap door for the attic. Out of curiosity, I asked what she was up to. She replied, "The next time a bear saunters into camp when we're alone, we're climbing up into the attic and we're playing cards until someone else arrives to rescue us." I am happy to report that we never had to resort to the attic!

North Knife Lake Lodge –

Canada's most exclusive fly-in fishing lodge.

Jalapeño Goose Breasts Suprême

Who hid the jalapeños? This is without a doubt our hunters' favorite. It is best made with tender young breasts. We do the preparation in the kitchen but Stewart, our camp manager, actually finishes them off on the barbecue. As he told the camera crew from ESPN when they were filming him at the barbecue, "The girls in the kitchen might call these Jalapeño Goose Breasts but we fellows call them Goose Boobies and they are delectable."

> **young goose breasts**
> **soy sauce**
> **fresh garlic cloves, crushed**
> **pickled jalapeño peppers and juice**
> **bacon drippings**

1. Use approximately 3 breasts per person. Put a single layer of goose breasts in a glass or plastic dish (a plastic ice-cream pail works well).
2. Spread with 2 crushed garlic cloves and pour over ¼ cup (60 mL) soy sauce.
3. Add another layer of breasts, crushed garlic and soy sauce until all breasts have been used. Be sure that the soy sauce almost covers the meat.

At Dymond Lake we usually put the breasts in the marinade* very early in the morning and leave them to marinate* all day . . . but early in the morning at Dymond lake is about 6:00 a.m., since we serve breakfast at 5:00 a.m. If you are like us and not too keen on being up at that hour of the morning, we would suggest that you marinate them overnight.

4. About an hour before serving, remove the breasts from the marinade and put a small slit on each side of the breast with a sharp knife. Into each of these slits stuff a small slice of pickled jalapeño pepper.
5. Now pile the breasts back into the dish or onto a tray to be taken out to the barbecue. On the tray put a small dish of melted bacon drippings and a dish of jalapeño juice from the pickle jar. You will also need a pair of tongs, a pastry brush and a small knife to check for doneness.
6. Barbecue the breasts over medium-high heat, brushing with bacon drippings and jalapeño juice until medium (still pink in the middle), about 4-6 minutes per side. Do not overcook.

SERVING SUGGESTION: We serve this with Marie's Wild Rice Casserole, page 126, Onion Salad, page 123, Broccoli Salad, page 115, fresh rolls (of course) and any one of our great desserts.

* *MARINADE OR MARINATE? Marinate is an action and marinade is what you do it in!*

See photograph on page 17.

Goose Fajitas

This is a delicious Mexican twist for serving goose or duck. Our guys just love it! If you like it a little hotter simply throw in a little hot sauce, or serve it with jalapeño peppers.

2 lbs.	goose OR duck breasts	1 kg
½ cup	butter OR margarine	125 mL
2	green peppers, chopped	2
1 cup	chopped onion	250 mL
½ cup	sliced fresh mushrooms	125 mL
1 tsp.	DLS* OR seasoned pepper	5 mL
1 cup	ketchup	250 mL
¼ cup	Pick-A-Peppa Sauce (chutney works)	60 mL
2 tbsp.	Worcestershire Sauce	30 mL
	soft tortillas OR pita pockets	
	sour cream	
	chopped green onions	
	chopped tomato	

1. Cut the goose or duck breasts in thin strips and sauté in half of the butter until just cooked. Slightly rare is okay.
2. Remove the meat and sauté the peppers, onions and mushrooms in the remainder of the butter. Sprinkle with seasoning.
3. Return the meat to the pan, add the ketchup, Pick-A-Peppa and Worcestershire and simmer for 5 minutes.
4. Roll up the goose vegetable mixture in the soft tortillas and serve with sour cream, chopped green onions and chopped tomatoes. You can also serve it in pita pockets for a nice change.

Serves 8.

* *Dymond Lake Seasoning*

HUNTER "Hey, don't shoot. Your gun isn't loaded yet.
PARTNER "Can't help that: the bird won't wait!"

Mushroom Goose

(HELEN) This is another winner for wild goose and again it uses the legs and breasts, though sometimes we choose to use all breasts. This was one of the original recipes I used at the hunting lodge back before the dawn of time and we are still using it with the approval of our hunters.

1 cup	flour	250 mL
1 tsp.	DLS* OR ½ tsp. (2 mL) seasoned pepper	5 mL
¼ tsp.	garlic powder	1 mL
½ tsp.	salt	2 mL
	legs and breasts of 4 birds OR the equivalent	
19 oz.	can mushroom soup	540 mL
10 oz.	can mushrooms with liquid	284 mL
½ cup	dry white wine	125 mL

1. Mix the first 5 ingredients together in a sturdy plastic bag. Shake the legs and breasts in the flour mixture.
2. Now here you have a choice. You can either brown the goose pieces in about ¼" (1 cm) of vegetable oil in a frying pan or put a small amount of oil on a baking sheet, place the goose pieces on it and throw them in the oven for 20 minutes at 400°F (200°C), turning once after 10 minutes. This is especially handy if you are doing large amounts.
3. Place the browned pieces in a heavy roaster.
4. Whisk the soup, mushrooms with liquid and white wine together and pour over goose pieces in roaster.
5. Cover and bake for 3 hours at 325°F (160°C). Stir at least twice during baking. If the sauce is too thick you can thin it with a little milk before serving.

Serves 6

* *Dymond Lake Seasoning.*

SERVING SUGGESTION: This is great with Marie's Wild Rice Casserole Suprême, page 126, Cranberry Sauce, page 198, Mandarin Orange Salad, page 120, a vegetable of your choice, fresh rolls and Cranberry Cake with Hot Butter Sauce, page 168.

FREEZING HINT: We remove the goose legs and breasts and pack them in 32 oz. (1 L) juice boxes, fill them with water so that meat is completely covered and then freeze them. When you thaw them out there is no freezer burn and they taste as fresh as the day they were harvested.

  Moose, Goose & Things That Swim

Goose Pie

We have asked for the legs and breasts of 2 geese but we often use the equivalent in legs if we have used up the breasts in other dishes. As a testimony to how good this pie is, we once had a hunter, named Bernie, eat almost 2 whole 10" (25 cm) goose pies by himself. It is also one of the dishes our repeat customers insist on every year. It is great served with Cranberry Sauce, page 198, or a nice chili sauce, tossed salad and crusty rolls. Just sit back and listen to the raves!

	legs and breasts of 2 geese	
½ cup	chopped onions	125 mL
4	beef bouillon cubes (4 tsp. [20 mL])	4
1	garlic clove, minced OR ¼ tsp. (1 mL) garlic powder	1
1 tsp.	Worcestershire sauce	5 mL
2 tbsp.	DLS*	30 mL
2 cups	diced potatoes	500 mL
1 cup	diced carrots	250 mL
¼ cup	flour	60 mL
1 cup	cold water	250 mL
10"	pie shell, uncooked, see pages 184, 185	25 cm

1. Place the first 6 ingredients in a large Dutch oven and cover with water. Simmer until the meat falls off the leg bones, about 3-4 hours. Let cool, remove meat from bones. Discard any meat that is still tough. That bird was too old! Chop up the breasts if they have not already fallen apart. Return the meat to the broth in the Dutch oven and add the vegetables.
2. Cook until vegetables are tender, about 30 minutes. Taste to check the seasoning and add a little salt or more DLS* to taste.
3. Blend the flour into the cold water, shaking it in a jar or using a hand blender. Stir into the pie filling; simmer and stir for about 2 minutes.
4. Pour into uncooked pie shell. Cover with top crust, cut slits to allow the steam to escape and bake at 425°F (220°C) for 10 minutes. Lower heat to 375° (190°C) and bake for an additional 40 minutes.
5. This pie freezes very well, baked or unbaked. If unbaked, thaw it before baking and increase the final baking time if necessary — we like it to be bubbling hot in the middle with a nicely browned crust. If baked, just heat through until hot and bubbly.

Serves 2-4 hungry hunters, or a family of 4-6.

VARIATION: We sometimes add ½ cup (125 mL) diced turnips and a 10 oz. (284 mL) can of mushrooms.

* *For Dymond Lake Seasoning substitute 1 tsp. (5mL) seasoned pepper, 1 tsp. (5mL) celery salt, 1 tbsp. (15 mL) parsley, ½ tsp. (2 mL) oregano, ½ tsp. (2 mL) basil, ½ tsp. (2 mL) thyme and salt to taste.*

Oven-Roasted Goose

We rarely choose to roast a wild goose as a whole bird since it tends to be some-what dry, and unless you know that it is young, it can be tough. The following method is guaranteed moist, tender and tasty!

	legs and breasts from 4 geese	
¼ cup	melted bacon drippings	60 mL
¼ cup	Louisiana Hot Sauce	60 mL
1 tbsp.	DLS* OR 1 tsp. (5 mL) each salt and seasoned pepper	15 mL

1. Place goose legs and breasts in a shallow roasting pan.
2. Drizzle with melted bacon drippings, Louisiana Hot Sauce and sprinkle with DLS*.
3. Place in a 450°F (230°C) oven for 15 minutes to brown. Cover, turn oven down to 350°F (180°C) and continue roasting for 2½-3 hours.
4. Thicken the juice with flour and water for a nice gravy.

* *Dymond Lake Seasoning*

SERVING SUGGESTIONS: We have also used goose roasted in this way in sand-wiches. Just remove the goose from the bones, chop it and add mayonnaise and seasonings.

A man bought a retriever and took him hunting. To his aston-ishment, the dog one day chased a goose right across a little pond. Instead of swimming the pond, the dog just ran across the surface of the water. The astonished dog owner invited a friend to observe the miracle, and was disappointed when the retriever's accomplishment failed to elicit any compliment.

"Well, what do you think of my dog?" the owner prodded.

"He can't swim," the friend answered.

Fish Balls

This is one of Mike's concoctions, see page 30, that we love to use as a taste teaser. He has handed the recipe on to us but whenever he is at the lodge we let him prepare it. This recipe uses cooked lake trout or pike so we usually freeze some after we have it baked for dinner. We serve this with either seafood sauce or Shari's Honey Dill Sauce, page 197.

	vegetable oil for deep-frying	
1 cup	flaked cooked fish	250 mL
1 cup	mashed potatoes	250 mL
2	eggs	2
½ cup	fine cracker crumbs	125 mL
2 tbsp.	DLS*	30 mL
1 tsp.	dried dillweed	5 mL
¼ cup	Parmesan cheese	60 mL
½ cup	fine cracker crumbs	125 mL

1. Heat the vegetable oil in a deep-fryer or heavy pot to 375°F (190°C). It should be at a depth of about 3" (7 cm) in the heavy pot or follow the manufacturer's recommendation for the deep-fryer.
2. Mix the next 7 ingredients together well. Form into 1" (2.5 cm) balls and roll in the second measurement of cracker crumbs, to coat the fish balls.
3. Drop the fish balls carefully into the hot oil and fry until a deep golden brown. This takes only 3-4 minutes. Drain and serve.

Makes 4 dozen.

SERVING SUGGESTIONS: We like to put a small bowl of sauce in the middle of a platter and surround it with fish balls. Looks great and tastes great!

* *For Dymond Lake Seasoning substitute 1 tsp. (5 mL) seasoned pepper, ½ tsp. (2 mL) salt, ¼ tsp. (1 mL) oregano, 1 tsp. (5 mL) celery flakes, 1 tbsp. (15 mL) parsley flakes.*

See photograph on page 103.

"How many fish have you caught, mister?" asked a boy, seeing an old man fishing on the banks of a stream.

"Well, son." answered the aged angler thoughtfully, "if I catch this one I'm after, and two more, then I'll have three."

Doug's Smoked Fish

(HELEN) You will notice that my husband Doug's name is conspicuous by its absence on the recipes in this cookbook. He does shine in 2 areas of cooking (I use the term loosely) — firstly, in making my first cup of tea of the day and delivering it to me in bed (in the off season) AND in making this smoked fish. If you have access to a smoker, this recipe is for you. We serve it as an hors d'oeuvre with crackers, use it in our Trout Pâté or just mix it up with mayonnaise for a great sandwich. It also makes fine gifts for those people who can't make it themselves.

P.S. Marie's husband's name is Gary — see if you find IT on any of the recipes!

1 cup	salt	250 mL
1 cup	brown sugar	250 mL
4-6	garlic cloves, minced, OR 1 tbsp. (15 mL) garlic powder	4-6
1	onion, minced, OR 2 tbsp. (30 mL) onion powder	1
¼ tsp.	allspice	1 mL
1 tbsp.	DLS* (optional)	15 mL
2 cups	boiling water	500 mL
2 qts.	cold water	2 L
4-6	fish fillets, skin on	4-6

1. Mix the salt, brown sugar, garlic, onion, allspice, DLS*, if using, and boiling water until the sugar and salt are dissolved.
2. Add an additional 2 quarts (2 L) of very cold water to cool it. Let cool to room temperature and then add the fish fillets, turning to be sure they are well coated with brine. Add a bit more water if necessary.
3. Place in a cool place and marinate for 12-24 hours.
4. Remove fillets from the brine and place on racks. Place in your smoker, skin side down, and follow the manufacturer's instructions. Doug uses the lowest heat possible for 8-10 hours. He likes to rescue the fish while it is still moist.

Yield: 4-6 smoked fillets.

SERVING SUGGESTION: Serve with plain crackers as an hors d'oeuvre or use in Smoked Trout Pâté, page 100.

NOTE: At North Knife we generally use lake trout and whitefish for smoking. You can try whatever you have.

* Dymond Lake Seasoning adds some zip to the fish, but it is not essential.

Smoking — A Dissertation by Doug

I think a few words need to be said about the smoking process and the selection of the wood used for the smoking.

The method I use most is called the Hot Smoke Method, which generally means that the fire or heat used to produce the smoke is in the same smoker as the fish. The Cold Smoke Method generally uses a larger container and the fire for producing the smoke is outside the container with a tube or pipe to carry the smoke (without heat) into the container (smoker).

As we used a lot of cherry wood in building North Knife Lake Lodge, we had a lot of sawdust and scraps which we saved just to be used for smoking. We also import the traditional hickory and the more exotic apple wood, as well as using our native willow which does an excellent job, too. A mixture of sawdust and chips offers a fairly lengthy burn, especially if put in damp. As propane is cheaper and more portable at our lodges, we have converted our smoker to propane, with the burner from a small water heater. I adjust the flame as low as possible and set a pie plate or 9" (23 cm) square baking pan of sawdust and chips on top, replacing the sawdust every 4 hours (only once if doing an 8-hour smoke). By smoking with the skin side down, the thicker portions of the fillet remain nice and moist while the belly portions are somewhat drier. This works well for us as some of our guests prefer a drier product while others enjoy the moist.

Cheddar-Baked Fish Fillets

(HELEN) This is my daughter Jeannie's recipe. She cooked her first turkey dinner at age 14. She went on to even bigger and better things and became quite an accomplished cook. She and her husband, Mike, run North Knife for us during the month of September while Doug and I are at Dymond Lake.

2 lbs.	Northern Pike fillets OR substitute pickerel OR lake trout	1 kg
1 cup	shredded medium Cheddar cheese	250 mL
1	large tomato, thinly sliced	1
½ tsp.	dried basil	2 mL
½ tsp.	dried oregano	2 mL
1 tsp.	DLS* OR ¼ tsp. (1 mL) seasoned salt and ½ tsp. (2 mL) seasoned pepper	5 mL

1. Arrange rinsed and dried fish fillets in a single layer in a 9 x 13" (23 x 33 cm) baking dish. Top with cheese, tomato slices and seasonings.
2. Bake in a preheated 375°F (190°C) oven for 15 minutes, or until fish flakes easily.

Serves 4-6.

* Dymond Lake Seasoning

Marie's Fish Chowder

Marie introduced us to this while she and Gary were living in Churchill. It became a regular lunch at the hunting lodge and a great "quicky" lunch on those rare occasions at North Knife when the weather brought the fishermen in for lunch .

¼ cup	butter OR margarine	60 mL
½ cup	chopped onions	125 mL
½ cup	chopped celery	125 mL
½ cup	diced carrots	125 mL
2 cups	diced raw potatoes	500 mL
1 tsp.	salt	5 mL
1 tbsp.	DLS*	15 mL
1 lb.	fish fillets, in bite-sized cubes	450 g
2 cups	cream OR evaporated milk	500 mL

1. Melt butter or margarine in heavy saucepan but do not brown. Add the onions and celery and sauté until limp. Add the carrots, potatoes, salt, DLS* and enough boiling water to just barely cover the vegetables. Cover and simmer 10-15 minutes, until tender.
2. Add the cubed fish and cook 5 minutes longer.
.   Add the cream or milk and heat through but do not boil.

Serves 4.

SERVING SUGGESTION: Serve with our Bannock, page 50, and sliced cheese.

* For Dymond Lake Seasoning substitute steak spice to taste.*

See photograph on page 69.

Crispy Fried Fish

	vegetable oil for frying	
6	fish fillets (cut into approx. 18 pieces)	6
½ cup	flour	125 mL
1 tbsp.	DLS* OR 1 tsp. (5 mL) seasoned pepper and ½ tsp. (2 mL) seasoned salt	15 mL
1 tsp.	garlic powder	5 mL
½ tsp.	salt	2 mL

1. Heat ¼" (1 cm) vegetable oil in a heavy frying pan.
2. In a bowl or bag, combine the flour, DLS*, garlic powder and salt.
3. Dredge the fish pieces in the flour mixture and fry them in the hot oil until crisp and golden brown on both sides, about 2-3 minutes per side.

SERVING SUGGESTIONS: Serve with Mustard Dill Sauce, page 33, or use fried fish to make Fish Burgers. Top your burger with Mustard Dill Sauce, tomatoes, raw onions, mozzarella or Cheddar cheese.

* Dymond Lake Seasoning*

Moose, Goose & Things That Swim

Gail's Maple-Marinated Fish Fillets

(HELEN) This wonderful recipe came via my daughter's mother-in-law who, coincidentally, with her husband ran a fishing lodge in northern Saskatchewan for years.

2 lbs.	fish fillets (we like pickerel OR northern pike but any firm white-fleshed fish will do)	1 kg
1 cup	maple syrup	250 mL
	oil for deep-frying	
¾ cup	flour	175 mL
¼ cup	cornstarch	60 mL
2 tsp.	baking powder	10 mL
1 tsp.	salt	5 mL
¾ cup	water	175 mL

1. Cut the fish fillets into serving-sized pieces and place in a shallow baking dish. Pour the maple syrup over, cover and refrigerate overnight.
2. Preheat oil for deep-frying to 375°F (190°C).
3. Mix flour, cornstarch, baking powder and salt in a bowl. Add water and beat with a wooden spoon until smooth. If it is too stiff to coat well, just add a bit more water.
4. Dip the fish fillets in the batter and deep-fry until golden brown.

Serves 4-6.

SERVING SUGGESTION: Serve this for breakfast with French toast and fruit salad. Give the salad an extra lift by adding just a touch of icing sugar and a dash of Mexican vanilla.

We thank thee, Lord, for happy hearts,
For rain and sunny weather,
We thank thee, Lord, for this our food,
And that we are together.
Emilie Fendall Johnson

Mike's Beer Batter Fish

When Mike (who later became Helen's son-in-law) first came to work for us he spent the first month at North Knife with Doug getting ready for the first guests. When Doug first hits North Knife in the spring he eats nothing but fresh fish for at least the first two weeks and consequently that is what whoever is with him gets to eat. Mike not only ate fish but learned to cook it as well and this is one of the recipes he came up with. It wasn't until a year later that we were having dinner with Mike's folks and Doug mentioned how he and Mike had enjoyed eating all this fresh fish that Mike's mother said, "but Mike doesn't like fish." He had learned to like it that summer — I guess he thought it was a case of like it or starve!

	oil for deep-frying	
2 lbs.	**fish fillets, any type of firm white-fleshed fish, pike and pickerel work well**	**1 kg**
1½ cups	**flour**	**375 mL**
1 tbsp.	**DLS* OR ½ tsp. (2 mL) salt and 1 tsp. (5 mL) pepper**	**15 mL**
12 oz.	**can beer**	**355 mL**
2 tsp.	**dillweed**	**10 mL**
½ tsp.	**salt**	**2 mL**
1	**egg**	**1**

1. Heat the vegetable oil in your deep-fryer or a large heavy Dutch oven to 375°F (190°C). You should have about 3" (7 cm) of oil.
2. Cut the fillets into serving pieces.
3. To make the batter, in a medium-sized bowl, whisk together the remaining ingredients with a wire whisk until smooth.
4. Drop fish pieces into the batter and then into the hot oil. Fry until deep golden brown, on both sides, turning once. Drain for just a minute on a wire rack placed over a cookie sheet.

Serves 6 hungry men or their equivalent.

SERVING SUGGESTION: Serve with a prepared seafood sauce or Shari's Honey Dill Sauce, page 197. This recipe goes very well with Parmesan Potatoes, page 129, and Creamy Green Coleslaw, page 124.

* Dymond Lake Seasoning

See photograph on page 121.

Winnie's Sweet 'N' Sour Fish

(HELEN) Winston came to work for us in 1991. He was our first Japanese fishing guide and brought a new element to the operation. Not only is he a first class guide but he is somewhat of a chef and he is dynamite in the garnishing department! After he had been around for a couple of weeks, I kept finding him lurking in my pantry. Now the pantry is just not where most of our guides hang out. Finally, one day I asked if there was anything he needed. "Well" he said, "I need the ingredients for sweet 'n' sour fish." This was a new one to me but I agreed to let him raid the pantry as long as I got to taste the end result. This recipe has since become a standard at shore lunches as well as a regular feature at the goose camp, and for company at home for both Marie and me.

Sweet 'N' Sour Sauce:

½ cup	soy sauce	125 mL
½ cup	ketchup	125 mL
½ cup	dry white wine	125 mL
½ cup	sugar	125 mL
½ cup	vinegar	125 mL
2 lbs.	fish fillets	1 kg
1 cup	flour	250 mL
2 tbsp.	DLS* OR 1 tsp. (5 mL) each salt, seasoned pepper, celery salt	30 mL
¼ tsp.	garlic powder	1 mL
1 cup	green pepper, in large cubes	250 mL
½ cup	onions, in large cubes	125 mL
8 oz.	can pineapple chunks	250 g

1. Whisk all the sauce ingredients together and set aside.
2. The fish can be pike, pickerel, orange roughy, sole or any firm, white-fleshed fish. Cut into serving-sized pieces.
3. Mix flour, DLS* and garlic powder.
4. Dredge fish in flour mixture and fry in ¼" (1 cm) medium hot vegetable oil until golden brown and crisp, about 3-4 minutes per side. Remove to a wire rack placed over a tray to drain.
5. Quickly drain the oil from the pan and wipe it out. Add 2 tbsp. (30 mL) fresh oil and stir-fry peppers and onions until tender-crisp.
6. Add the pineapple, fish and the sauce. Stir gently to mix; bring to a boil; simmer 2-3 minutes.

Serves 4-6.

SERVING SUGGESTION: Serve alone as an hors d'oeuvre or with rice and a fresh, crisp salad for a nice lunch or dinner.

* Dymond Lake Seasoning.

Stuffed Baked Lake Trout

(HELEN) This recipe is a good example of how much Marie and I think alike even though she is basically left-brained and I am right-brained. We were discussing the stuffing we each put in our lake trout. I said that I made a rice stuffing with bread cubes in it and she said that she did too. And then she said that she put lemon juice and lemon rind in it and I said that I did too! And this was a recipe that we both used years before we ever met. We had both just kind of thrown it together and decided we liked it.

4-6 lb.	lake trout	2-3 kg
½ cup	chopped onion	125 mL
¼ cup	chopped celery	60 mL
¼ cup	butter OR margarine	60 mL
2	slices of bread, cubed (white OR whole-wheat)	2
1½ cups	cooked white rice	375 mL
1 tbsp.	lemon juice	15 mL
½ tsp.	grated lemon peel (¼ tsp. [1 mL], if dried)	2 mL
¼ tsp.	dried rosemary	1 mL
¼ tsp.	dried thyme	1 mL
½ tsp.	salt	2 mL
1 tsp.	DLS* OR ½ tsp. (2 mL) pepper	5 mL

1. Prepare the fish for stuffing
2. Sauté the onion and celery in the butter until soft.
3. Cube the bread and put in a bowl. Add the cooked rice, lemon juice, lemon peel, rosemary, thyme, salt and DLS* or substitute. Add the onion and celery and mix well.
4. Place the trout in the middle of a large piece of foil. Pack the stuffing into the cavity. Sprinkle the top with DLS* or salt and pepper; wrap in the foil and place on a baking sheet.
5. Place in a 400°F (200°C) oven and bake for 12 minutes per inch (2.5 cm) of thickness, measured at the thickest part of the back. Check for doneness by inserting a small knife at the thickest point. If the fish lifts off easily, it is done.
6. Remove stuffing to a bowl and keep warm.
7. Use a knife to lift the top skin off the fish and a large spoon to lift the fish off the backbone. Lift out the backbone and lift the rest of the fish off the bottom skin. Work quickly, as the fish tends to cool down in record time. If necessary, keep warm in the oven.

Serves 6.

SERVING SUGGESTIONS: This is delicious served with Mustard Dill Sauce, page 34, or Provençale Sauce, page 34, and teamed up with Sweet 'N' Sassy Potatoes, page 132.

* Dymond Lake Seasoning

Moose, Goose & Things That Swim

Baked Lake Trout

This has been a real favorite at the hunting lodge. We let them know at North Knife that we want to serve lake trout for dinner the next day and with a little prayer and some luck the airplane arrives with the chef's catch of the day in time for us to serve it for dinner — talk about fresh!! We always have a backup plan in case of bad weather though. You can't have sixteen hungry hunters waiting for dinner and nothing to serve them. Now the guides have added this dish to their shore lunch menu at North Knife so our fishermen get to enjoy it too. After all, they catch 'em!

4-5 lb.	whole lake trout	2-2.2 kg
	DLS* OR salt and seasoned pepper	
	onion slices	
¼ cup	dry white wine	60 mL
	lemon slices	

1. Dress** a whole lake trout (with head and tail removed if you prefer although they add to the aesthetic value if you are going to take it to the table to serve). Place the fish on a large sheet of greased foil.
2. Sprinkle the cavity and the outside of the fish liberally with DLS* or salt and pepper.
3. Place a row of sliced onions in the cavity and then pour in the dry white wine.
4. Wrap well in greased foil, place on a baking sheet and bake at 400°F (200°C) for 10 minutes per inch (2.5 cm) of thickness (measured at the thickest part of the back). Bake just until the meat at the thickest point flakes easily. Do not over bake!

SERVING SUGGESTIONS: Place whole fish on a platter and garnish with lemon slices. To serve, use a knife to remove the skin and then lift the fish off the bones. A 4-5 lb. (2-2.2 kg) fish will serve 6-8. Serve with one of the sauces on page 34.

* *Dymond Lake Seasoning*
** *A dressed fish is one that has been gutted and cleaned. What did you think it was?*

Provençale Sauce

| ½ cup | butter | 125 mL |
| 1 tbsp. | Provençale* | 15 mL |

1. Melt butter and add Provençale. Mix well and serve.

* *Provençale, or Herbs de Provence, is a mixture of herbs and spices. You will find it with the other seasonings in your supermarket, or substitute a mixture of basil, thyme, rosemary, fennel seed, parsley, oregano, sage, summer savory, marjoram, lavender.*

Mustard Dill Sauce

1 cup	mayonnaise OR salad dressing	250 mL
¼ cup	prepared mustard	60 mL
1 tsp.	dried dillweed	5 mL

1. Mix well and serve.

See photograph on page 121.

By Hook or by Crook!

A certain dentist from Southern Ontario was a guest at the Lodge one summer. He was, in fact, a friend from years ago in Churchill, or I wouldn't take it upon myself to put this tale in print. It was a fine day, and we had all gone out for a shore lunch — that means that the guides got to do the cooking and Helen and I got a break. The fishing hadn't been great; so upon reaching the lunch spot, our dentist friend sought out the nearest rock and started casting. Still catching nothing, he ventured further along the shore, around a point of land and out of sight of all but one young lad. Suddenly there was a flurry of hooting and hollering, which aroused our interest and got us looking expectantly in the direction of the disturbance. Around the corner came the young lad, on the run, grinning near to splitting his face. It seemed that the dentist had been successful in hooking a fish — a big northern. In his exuberance, he yanked it out of the water with such force, that it looped towards him and hooked — of all places — in the crotch of his pants. I still can see him, though only in my imagination, with that big northern still dangling from the malplaced hook!

Moose, Goose & Things That Swim

Bread and Breakfast

At both the Lodges, we take pleasure in producing the best possible homemade bread products. So, whether we are serving breakfast, lunch or supper, part of the meal has come from this section.

No one ever refuses breakfast at the Lodges. When they know they have a long day of fishing or hunting ahead of them they have to eat to keep up their strength. I am sure you spouses who have hunting or fishing mates have heard all about what hard work it is, wink, wink. Well, I have a question for you. When was the last time you got up in the morning to a full-course breakfast, all prepared, wandered down to a boat where your guide was waiting to take care of your every whim for the day, relaxed while he prepared and cleaned up from your lunch and returned you to the Lodge in time for hors d'oeuvres and cocktails followed by a scrumptious dinner? Does that sound like hard work to you?

Just a word of advice, the next time you are invited to go fishing at a five-star lodge — say YES!

Baking With Yeast

Most, though not all, of the recipes in this section use yeast. Therefore, we would like to share some of the things we have learned, through experience, about baking with yeast.

Water Temperature: When using tap water in a bread recipe, the water should feel quite warm when tested on the inside of your wrist, but not hot! For those of you who are experienced bread makers this will sound very elementary, but the rest of you can learn from two who learned to make bread by trial and error on their own — it is important to the success of the product. Hot water destroys yeast.

Rising Techniques: When setting the dough in a warm place to rise, cover it with a cloth or tea towel. Helen also puts a piece of plastic over the dry cloth. She finds that it keeps the top of the dough from drying out and creates more warmth in the dough. Marie doesn't bother with it and her results are just as good so go with whichever method you prefer.

For Evenly Baked Breads: When using 2 racks of your oven at the same time, switch the pans from top to bottom, and visa versa, halfway through the baking time.

Oven Temperature: Always use a preheated oven.

Oil vs. Butter or Margarine: When making bread & buns, we use oil instead of butter or margarine. We do this for convenience and find that it works just as well.

Quality of Flour: Over the years, we have tried many kinds of flour. We have found no difference in the taste and quality of our breads, whether we used a name brand or a no-name brand. Occasionally, there was a slight difference in the degree of whiteness.

Types of Yeast: Our recipes are all written for the use of INSTANT YEAST, but quick-rising yeast works just as well. For QUICK-RISING YEAST, take 1 cup (250 mL) of the water called for in the recipe, and put it in a small bowl with 1 tsp. (5 mL) sugar. Sprinkle the yeast over the water, letting it fall from a distance of at least 6" (15 cm). This forces the yeast to go beneath the surface of the water where it dissolves more easily. Do not stir. Put in a warm place to sit until yeast mixture has become bubbly, about 5 minutes. Add to recipe as directed.

Freezing and Thawing Tips: Break buns apart and slice bread before freezing. This way, you thaw only what you want to use immediately. Frozen slices of bread can be toasted without thawing first. To thaw a frozen loaf of bread, put it in the microwave, uncovered, on high heat for 2 minutes. 1 bun takes 30 seconds.

Greasing Pans or Working Surfaces: When the recipe calls for greased pans or surfaces, we use a nonstick cooking spray that is environmentally safe.

Shaping Buns: Spread your fingers, palm side down, into the shape of a spider; place your curved fingers over the dough and move your hand in circular motions on the greased surface, putting a little pressure on the dough. With practice, you will quickly shape the dough into a smooth ball. With more practice, you will be doing it with both hands at once!

Bread & Breakfast

English Muffins

At the Lodges, if you're fortunate enough to have Eggs Benedict, you also get our homemade English Muffins. These take a little longer than running to the store, (unless the store is 150 miles away) but they're worth it.

2 cups	warm water	500 mL
⅓ cup	white sugar	75 mL
1 tbsp.	salt	15 mL
6½ cups	flour	1.625 L
2 tbsp.	instant yeast*	30 mL
2	eggs	2
⅓ cup	shortening	75 mL
	cornmeal	

1. Combine water, sugar and salt. Add 2 cups (500 mL) flour and yeast. Beat for 2 minutes.
2. Add eggs and shortening. Beat for 1 minute.
3. Work in remaining flour and let dough rest in the bowl for 20 minutes.
4. Roll dough to ½" (1.3 cm) thickness. Cut with a 3-4" (7-10 cm) cutter. (A glass or empty can works well.)
5. Place on an ungreased baking sheet which has been sprinkled with cornmeal. Sprinkle a little cornmeal over the muffins. Cover with a cloth and let rise for 45 minutes.
6. Preheat an ungreased electric frying pan to 375°F (190°C). Sprinkle the pan with cornmeal and cook muffins for 7-8 minutes each side. They should be browned and sound hollow when done.

Makes 2 dozen muffins.

* *See note on YEAST on page 36.*

We thank Thee for our daily bread
Let, also, Lord, our souls be fed
O, Bread of Life, from day to day
Sustain us on our homeward way.
                    The Fekhardt Family.

White Buns

This may be one of our most requested recipes. This is a light, moist bun that rises exceptionally well, and sells like hot-cakes at a bake sale! We know that our guests appreciate fresh buns for dinner every night.

5 cups	lukewarm water	1.25 L
6 tbsp.	white sugar*	90 mL
1 tbsp.	salt*	15 mL
½ cup	vegetable oil	125 mL
2	eggs, room temperature**	2
13 cups	flour (approximately)	3.25 L
2 tbsp.	instant yeast***	30 mL

1. In a large mixing bowl, combine water, sugar, salt, oil, eggs, 5 cups (1.25 L) flour and yeast. Mix with an electric mixer or wire whisk.
2. Gradually add remaining flour and work into the dough either with a dough hook on your mixer or by hand. If by hand, turn dough out onto a well-floured surface and work flour into dough with a kneading motion, until dough feels soft, smooth and velvety, 8-10 minutes. You may need MORE or LESS flour.
3. Shape dough into a ball, place in a large, well-greased bowl, turning dough to grease surface. Cover with a cloth or a piece of plastic***. Put in a warm place and let rise until doubled in size, about an hour.
4. Punch down dough and turn out onto WELL-GREASED surface. With a bread knife, cut dough into 4 equal parts.
5. Working with one quarter at a time, cut each quarter of dough into 12 pieces. Shape each piece into a bun***. Place buns 1" (2.5 cm) apart on a greased baking sheet or pan. Cover and let rise in a warm place until buns have at least doubled in size, about an hour.
6. Bake in a 350°F (180°C) oven for 20-25 minutes. Turn baked buns out of pans onto a cooling rack.

Makes 4 dozen large buns.

SESAME BUNS: Just before popping the buns in the oven, brush them with a mixture of 1 egg white and 1 tbsp. (15 mL) water. Sprinkle with sesame seeds.

* Amounts of salt and sugar are flexible. If you want less of each, reduce salt to 2 tsp. (10 mL) and sugar to ¼ cup (60 mL).
** To get eggs to room temperature quickly, place them in a cup of hot tap water for a couple of minutes, BEFORE cracking them.
*** See notes on YEAST, RISING TECHNIQUES, SHAPING BUNS and freezing techniques on page 36.

 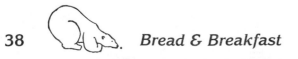

Cinnamon Buns

Is there anyone who doesn't like cinnamon buns? We like to serve them before early morning flights and for groups that arrive midmorning. We also try to keep some in the freezer to impress surprise visitors.

	warm water	
	brown sugar	
	cinnamon	
	raisins (optional)	
	ingredients for White Buns, page 38	
½ cup	icing sugar	125 mL
2 tsp.	milk	10 mL

1. Follow recipe for white buns, steps 1 through 3, on previous page.
2. Punch down dough and turn out onto a WELL-GREASED surface. With a bread knife, cut dough into 2 equal parts.
3. Working with one half at a time, roll out the dough into a rectangle, 12 x 24" (30 x 60 cm). Use a rolling pin.
4. Cover the surface of the dough with warm water*.
5. Sprinkle brown sugar over the water. Be generous and make sure that the whole surface area is covered.
6. Sprinkle liberally with cinnamon. Scatter raisins over, if desired.
7. Rolling from the 24" (60 cm) end, roll dough into a 24" (60 cm) long log.
8. Cut log into 24 even slices. Place each slice, 1" (2.5 cm) apart, flat side down, on well-greased baking sheets with raised sides. You can also use 2, 9 x 13" (23 x 33 cm) cake pans. The buns will be closer together and will rise higher, rather than spreading out.
9. Cover buns and let rise in a warm place until doubled in size, about an hour.
10. Bake in a preheated 350°F (180°C) oven for 20-25 minutes. They are better under-cooked than over-cooked .
11. Turn baked buns out on a rack to cool. Be prepared for drips.

Makes 4 dozen cinnamon buns OR 2 dozen cinnamon and 2 dozen white buns.

SERVING SUGGESTIONS: Just before serving, drizzle with a thin icing made from ½ cup (125 mL) icing sugar and 2 tsp. (10 mL) milk.

* *We used to use melted butter in this step until we heard that the bakeries use water. Being skeptics, we tried doing half a batch each way and couldn't tell the difference. The choice is yours.*

Crusty Rolls

You've heard of a crusty character; this is a crusty roll. Both have hard exteriors, but are real softies inside.

2 cups	lukewarm water	500 mL
3 tbsp.	butter OR margarine, melted	45 mL
2 tbsp.	white sugar	30 mL
2 tsp.	salt	10 mL
5 cups	flour (approximately)	1.25 mL
1	egg white	1
1 tbsp.	yeast*	15 mL
1	egg white	1
1 tbsp.	water	15 mL
	sesame OR poppy seeds	

1. Combine water, butter, sugar, salt, 1¾ cups (425 mL) flour, egg white and yeast in a large mixing bowl. Beat until smooth.
2. Switch to a dough hook, if you have one, and add the rest of the flour, gradually. Knead until dough isn't too sticky to handle. If kneading by hand, add as much flour as you can in the bowl, then turn out onto a FLOURED surface, and work in the rest of the flour by hand, using a kneading motion. You may need MORE or LESS flour, but knead dough until it is smooth but not sticky, and bounces back when pressed, about 8-10 minutes.
3. Place in a greased bowl, turning to grease top of dough. Cover* and let rise in a warm place until double in bulk, about 45 minutes.
4. While you are waiting, prepare 2 cookie sheets by greasing them and sprinkling them with cornmeal.
5. Punch down dough and turn out on a greased surface. Divide dough in half. Form each half into a 9" (23 cm) roll. Cut each roll into 9 pieces. Form each piece into a smooth ball*.
6. Place balls about 3" (7 cm) apart on the prepared baking sheets. Cover and let rise in a warm place until doubled in bulk, about an hour.
7. When ready to bake, brush rolls with a mixture of 1 egg white and 1 tbsp. (15 mL) water. Slit tops with a sharp knife criss-cross fashion, and sprinkle with sesame or poppy seeds.
8. Bake in a hot oven, 400°F (200°C), for 15 minutes.
9. Remove rolls from baking sheets and cool on racks.

Makes 18 buns. Doubles well.

* *See notes on YEAST, RISING TECHNIQUES and SHAPING BUNS on page 36.*

Red River Bread

Each day at the Lodges begins with a breakfast that includes Red River Cereal. I doubt if many people realize that they are also eating cereal in their sandwiches and toast. That's because what began as an experiment to use up the leftover cereal turned into a tradition that we hope you will enjoy in your own homes.

4 cups	lukewarm water	1 L
6 tbsp.	white sugar*	90 mL
1 tbsp.	salt*	15 mL
½ cup	vegetable oil	125 mL
2 cups	cooked Red River cereal**(approximately)	500 mL
13 cups	flour (approximately)	3.25 L
2 tbsp.	instant yeast***	30 mL

1. In a large mixing bowl, combine water, sugar, salt, oil and cereal. If you don't have an automatic mixer, use a wire whisk and mix well.
2. Add 4 cups (1 L) of flour and the yeast. Mix well.
3. Switch to a dough hook, if you have one, and add the rest of the flour, gradually. Knead until dough isn't too sticky to handle. If kneading by hand, add as much flour as you can in the bowl, then turn out onto a FLOURED surface. Knead in the rest of the flour by hand. It may take a little MORE or a little LESS flour. Just knead the dough until it feels soft but not sticky, and bounces back when pressed, 8-10 minutes.
4. Shape dough into a ball, place in a large, well-greased bowl, turning dough to grease surface. Cover with a cloth***. Put in a warm place and let rise until doubled in size, about an hour.
5. Punch down dough and turn out onto a GREASED surface. With a bread knife, divide dough into 5 even portions. Shape each portion into a loaf, using a kneading motion. (Or use a rolling pin to roll out the dough, and then roll it into a loaf.) Whatever method you use, it might not LOOK perfect the first time, but you'll improve with practice.
6. Place loaves in well-greased 3 x 5 x 8" (7 x 13 x 20 cm) bread pans. Cover with a cloth. Let rise until bread has risen 1" (2.5 cm) above the pans, about an hour.
7. Remove cloth and bake loaves at 350°F (180°C) for 30 minutes.
8. Remove baked loaves from oven and turn out of pans onto a cooling rack. Loaves should be brown on bottom and sides as well as on top.

Makes 5 loaves.

* *Amounts of salt and sugar are flexible. If you want less of each, reduce salt to 2 tsp. (10 mL) and sugar to ¼ cup (60 mL).*

** *If making Red River Cereal from scratch, use 1 cup (250 mL) dry cereal, boiled in 3 cups (750 mL) of water. It makes more than 2 cups (500 mL), but you can use it all in this recipe.*

*** *See notes on YEAST and RISING TECHNIQUES on page 36.*

See photograph on page 121.

White or Brown Bread

Most cooks have their own bread recipe which has evolved with years of practice. Helen and I do basically the same thing — we throw a bunch of the same ingredients together and come out with a bread that tastes darn good! Only because that recipe would be a little difficult to follow, we've gone to the trouble of measuring — just for you.

White Bread

5 cups	water	1.25 L
6 tbsp.	white sugar*	90 mL
1 tbsp.	salt*	15 mL
½ cup	vegetable oil	125 mL
13 cups	flour	3.25 L
2 tbsp.	instant yeast**	30 mL

1. In a large mixing bowl, combine water, sugar, salt and oil. If you don't have an automatic mixer, use a wire whisk and mix well.
2. Add 4 cups (1 L) of flour and the yeast. Mix well.
3. Switch to a dough hook, if you have one, and add the rest of the flour, gradually. Knead until dough isn't too sticky to handle. If kneading by hand, add as much flour as you can in the bowl, then turn out onto a FLOURED surface, and work in the rest of the flour by hand, using a kneading motion. It may take a little MORE or a little LESS flour. Just knead the dough until it feels soft but not sticky, and bounces back when pressed, 8-10 minutes.
4. Shape dough into a ball, place in a large, well-greased bowl, turning dough to grease surface. Cover with a cloth**. Put in a warm place and let rise until doubled in size, about an hour.
5. Punch down dough, turn out onto a GREASED surface and cut into 5 equal pieces.
6. Shape dough into loaves, using a kneading motion. (It takes practice to get a smoothly shaped loaf. Don't get discouraged the first time. It won't affect the taste.)
7. Place loaves in well-greased 3 x 4 x 8" (7 x 10 x 20 cm) bread pans. Cover with a cloth. Let rise until bread has risen an inch (2.5 cm) above the pans, about an hour.
8. Remove cloth and bake loaves in a preheated 350°F (180°C) oven for 30 minutes.
9. Remove baked loaves from oven and turn out of pans onto a cooling rack. Loaves should be brown on bottom and sides as well as on top.

Makes 5 loaves.

* Amounts of salt and sugar are flexible. If you want less of each, reduce salt to 2 tsp. (10 mL) and sugar to ¼ cup (60 mL).

** See notes on YEAST and RISING TECHNIQUES on page 36.

Bread & Breakfast

Brown Bread

5 cups	water	1.25 L
6 tbsp.	white sugar*	90 mL
1 tbsp.	salt*	15 mL
½ cup	vegetable oil	125 mL
3 cups	whole-wheat flour**	750 mL
2 cups	rolled oats**	500 mL
8 cups	white flour	2 L
2 tbsp.	instant yeast***	30 mL

1. In a large mixing bowl, combine water, sugar, salt and oil. If you don't have an automatic mixer, use a wire whisk and mix well.
2. Add 2 cups (500 mL) whole-wheat flour, the rolled oats and yeast. Mix well.
3. Follow remaining directions for White Bread on page 42.

Makes 5 loaves.

* *Amounts of salt and sugar are flexible. If you want less of each, reduce salt to 2 tsp. (10 mL) and sugar to ¼ cup (60 mL).*

** *Amounts of whole-wheat flour and rolled oats are flexible. Graham flour may also be used for a cracked-wheat bread.*

*** *See notes on YEAST and RISING TECHNIQUES on page 36.*

Bread is a lovely thing to eat —
God bless the barley and the wheat;
A lovely thing to breathe is air —
God bless the sunshine everywhere;
The earth's a lovely place to know —
God bless the folks that come and go!
Alive's a lovely thing to be —
Giver of life — we say — bless Thee!

French Bread

Le pain français, c'est bon, n'est-ce pas? Okay, we'll give these instructions in English.

5 cups	lukewarm water	1.25 L
2 tbsp.	white sugar	30 mL
4 tsp.	salt	20 mL
2 tbsp.	melted butter OR vegetable oil	30 mL
12 cups	flour (approximately)	3 L
2 tbsp.	instant yeast*	30 mL
1	egg white	1
1 tbsp.	water	15 mL

1. In a large mixing bowl, combine water, sugar, salt and oil. If you don't have an automatic mixer, use a wire whisk and mix well.
2. Add 4 cups (4 L) of flour and the yeast. Mix well.
3. Switch to a dough hook, if you have one, and add the rest of the flour, gradually. Knead until dough isn't too sticky to handle. If kneading by hand, add as much flour as you can in the bowl, then turn out onto a FLOURED surface, and work in the rest of the flour by hand, using a kneading motion. It may take a little MORE or a little LESS flour. Just knead the dough until it feels soft but not sticky, and bounces back when pressed, 8-10 minutes.
4. Shape dough into a ball, place in a large, well-greased bowl, turning dough to grease surface. Cover with a cloth*. Put in a warm place and let rise until doubled in size, about an hour.
5. While you are waiting, prepare 2 cookie sheets by greasing them and sprinkling them with cornmeal.
6. Punch down dough and cut into 4 equal parts. Shape each quarter into a long loaf, about 15" (38 cm). You may want to use a rolling pin. Roll each quarter into a 10 x 15" (25 x 38 cm) rectangle. Beginning at a 15" (38 cm) side, roll up tightly, like a jelly roll. Seal edges well. Taper ends by rolling them gently back and forth.
7. Place loaves on prepared pans, 2 loaves to a pan. Let rise, UNCOVERED, in a warm place until doubled in size, about 1 hour.
8. Just before baking, make 4 diagonal cuts on the top of each loaf, with a sharp knife. Brush tops of loaves with the egg white/water mixture.
9. Bake in a preheated 375°F (190°C) oven for 30 minutes.
10. Remove baked loaves from pans and cool on racks.

Makes 4 loaves.

* *See notes on YEAST and RISING TECHNIQUES on page 36.*

See photograph on page 155.

Bread & Breakfast

French Toast

The simplest of breakfasts. Make it really special by serving it with Grand Marnier Sauce, page 198.

4	eggs, beaten	4
1 cup	milk	250 mL
1 tsp.	icing sugar	5 mL
½ tsp.	vanilla	2 mL
8-10	slices French bread, ¾" (2 cm) thick	8-10
	butter OR margarine	

1. In a shallow pan, combine eggs, milk, sugar and vanilla. Mix well.
2. In a frying pan or griddle, melt butter over medium heat.
3. Dip 1 slice of bread at a time into the egg mixture and let soak for a few seconds on each side. Lift out, letting excess mixture drip back into the pan.
4. Fry soaked bread for 1-2 minutes on each side, until golden brown, adding more butter to the griddle as needed.

Makes 8-10 pieces of French Toast.

SERVING SUGGESTION: Serve with bacon or sausage, a choice of maple syrup or Grand Marnier Sauce. Dress up your plate with a couple of orange slices.

NOTE: When cooking for a crowd, keep French Toast warm in a 150°F (70°C) oven.

Bless our hearts to hear
in the breaking of the bread
the song of the Universe.
Father John Guiliani

Trail Bread

We discovered this delightful recipe when preparing for a 5-day, Webber/Woolsey canoe trip. It is a heavy, unleavened bread, very nutritious, and it keeps for 2 weeks on the trail. You pull your canoe up on shore, get out the bread and a jar of peanut butter or honey and, presto, lunch is ready!

1 cup	butter OR margarine, softened	250 mL
½ cup	honey	125 mL
1	egg	1
1 cup	flour	250 mL
3½ cups	oatmeal (rolled oats)	875 mL
½ cup	dry milk powder	125 mL
⅔ cup	raisins	150 mL
½ cup	chopped dates	125 mL
½ cup	chopped OR sliced nuts	125 mL

1. In a large bowl, cream the butter and honey. Add the egg and blend well.
2. Mix together the flour, oatmeal and milk powder, and add it to the honey mixture.
3. Add the raisins, dates and nuts and mix well.
4. Spread batter in a WELL-GREASED 9 x 13" (23 x 33 cm) pan.
5. Bake at 300°F (150°C) for 45-50 minutes. The bread will be well bronzed when done.
6. Remove the trail bread from the pan and allow it to cool on a rack.
7. When cool, store the bread in an airtight container and hit the trail!

Makes a 9 x 13" (23 x 33 cm) panful.

Golden Corn Bread

A pleasant lunch bread, with soup, on a cold day. This is also very good with chili or stew.

1 cup	flour	250 mL
¼ cup	white sugar	60 mL
4 tsp.	baking powder	20 mL
¾ tsp.	salt	4 mL
1 cup	yellow cornmeal	250 mL
2	eggs	2
1 cup	milk	250 mL
¼ cup	vegetable oil	60 mL

Bread & Breakfast

Golden Corn Bread

Continued

1. In a large bowl, mix flour, sugar, baking powder, salt and cornmeal.
2. In a small bowl, beat eggs; add milk and oil.
3. Add liquids to cornmeal mixture. Stir with a fork until flour is just moistened. Batter may be lumpy.
4. Pour into greased 9" (23 cm) square pan. Bake at 425°F (220°C) for 20-25 minutes, or until done.

Makes a 9" (23 cm) panful.

SERVING SUGGESTION: Cut in squares and serve hot with butter. Maple syrup or honey are welcome additions to hot corn bread.

Baking Powder Cinnamon Rolls

Old-fashioned cinnamon rolls the quick and easy way.

2 cups	flour	500 mL
¼ cup	white sugar	60 mL
4 tsp.	baking powder	20 mL
½ tsp.	salt	2 mL
½ tsp.	cream of tartar	2 mL
½ cup	butter OR margarine, softened	125 mL
⅞ cup	milk	200 mL

Cinnamon Filling:

2 tbsp.	butter OR margarine, melted	30 mL
½ cup	sugar, brown OR white	125 mL
2 tbsp.	cinnamon	30 mL

1. In a large bowl, combine flour, sugar, baking powder, salt and cream of tartar. Using a pastry blender, cut butter into dry ingredients. Add milk, mixing with a fork just until evenly moistened.
2. On floured board, knead dough 3 or 4 times, then roll out dough into a 10 x 15" (25 x 38 cm) rectangle.
3. In a separate bowl, combine the filling ingredients and spread over the dough. Starting from a 15" (38 cm) side, roll up dough into a log and cut into 15, 1" (2.5 cm) pieces.
4. Place rolls in a greased 9 x 13" (23 x 33 cm) pan and bake at 425°F (220°C) for 20 minutes. Turn rolls out on a rack to cool.

Makes 15 rolls.

Traditional Tea Biscuits

The flaky layers in tea biscuits are what makes them so light and easy to break apart. You'll have hot biscuits in 20-25 minutes. Sounds good to me!

2¼ cups	flour	560 mL
4 tsp.	baking powder	20 mL
1 tsp.	salt	5 mL
½ cup	shortening	125 mL
1 cup	milk	250 mL

1. In a large bowl, mix flour, baking powder and salt. With a pastry blender, cut shortening into dry ingredients, until mixture is crumbly.
2. Add milk all at once and stir lightly with a fork, just until a soft sticky dough is formed. Do not overmix.
3. Turn out dough on a lightly floured surface and knead gently, 8-10 times. (That's what makes the flaky layers.)
4. Pat out dough to ½" (1.25 cm) thick. Cut into circles with a 1¾" (4.5 cm) cutter. A glass works fine.
5. Bake biscuits on an ungreased baking sheet at 450°F (230°C) for 12-15 minutes, or until light golden brown.

Makes 18-20 biscuits.

Sweet Biscuits or Scones

A sweet tea biscuit, if that's the way you prefer them.

2 cups	flour	500 mL
1 tsp.	salt	5 mL
1 tsp.	baking powder	5 mL
1 tsp.	baking soda	5 mL
1 tsp.	cream of tartar	5 mL
1 tbsp.	white sugar	15 mL
3 tbsp.	butter OR margarine	45 mL
1	egg	1
	milk	

Sweet Biscuits or Scones

Continued

1. Combine dry ingredients and cut in butter with a pastry blender, until pebbly.
2. Beat egg in a measuring cup and fill to 1 cup (250 mL) with milk. Add to dry ingredients and mix with a fork, just until evenly moistened.
3. Turn out dough on a floured board and knead lightly, 4-6 times.
4. Pat out dough to about ½" (1.3 cm) thickness. Cut with a 2" (5 cm) floured cookie cutter or cut into squares with knife.
5. Place biscuits on an ungreased baking sheet and bake at 400°F (200°C) for 10-15 minutes, or until lightly browned.

Makes 12 biscuits.

Cheese Biscuits

Occasionally, you want a change from traditional tea biscuits. A hint of cheese gives a tasty alternative. These drop biscuits are ideal for the busy cook.

2 cups	flour	500 mL
4 tsp.	baking powder	20 mL
½ tsp.	salt	2 mL
¾ cup	butter OR margarine	175 mL
2 cups	finely grated cheese*	500 mL
1 cup	water	250 mL

1. Put flour, baking powder and salt in a bowl. Add butter and cut in with pastry blender until fairly well blended. Small lumps are all right.
2. Add cheese and stir in with a fork, carefully separating any cheese that has lumped together.
3. Add water all at once and stir with a fork just until blended.
4. Drop batter by heaping tablespoons (about 25 mL) onto an ungreased baking sheet.
5. Bake at 450°F (230°C) for 10-12 minutes. Jagged peaks on the tops of the biscuits will be browned. Remove the biscuits from the tray immediately.

Makes 15 large biscuits.

SERVING SUGGESTION: Serve warm for an evening snack or to accompany a light lunch.

* *Use Cheddar or mozzarella or a mixture or experiment with any hard cheese. Cheese should be only loosely packed when measuring.*

Bannock

(MARIE) This tender and cake-like bannock recipe came from an Ojibwa woman by the name of Jo Beaucage who was a guest in my home about 25 years ago.

4 cups	flour	1 L
2 tbsp.	baking powder	30 mL
1 tsp.	salt	5 mL
1 cup	lard, melted	250 mL
2¼ cups	milk	560 mL

1. Mix flour, baking powder and salt in a large mixing bowl.
2. In a small saucepan, melt lard. Pour ½ cup (125 mL) melted lard into a 9" (23 cm) square baking pan.
3. Pour milk into the remaining ½ cup (125 mL) lard in the saucepan. It will sizzle a little. Heat just until warm.
4. Pour lard and milk into flour mixture and stir quickly, just until blended.
5. Spread batter gently in the prepared pan. Dip your fingers in the melted lard to prevent the dough from sticking to you.
6. Bake at 450°F (230°C) for 20-30 minutes. Turn out of pan and cut into squares to serve. Serve warm or cold.

Makes a 9" (23 cm) panful.

NOTE: For a 9 x 13" (23 x 33 cm) pan, we just increase the ingredients by half, e.g., 6 cups (1.5 L) flour, 3 tbsp. (45 mL) baking powder, 1½ tsp. (7 mL) salt, 3⅓ cups (825 mL) milk, 1½ cups (375 mL) melted lard.

Bread and Breakfast

Camping Bannock

(MARIE) When going on a canoe trip or back-packing, we make up bannock mix ahead of time. All we have to do before it hits the frying pan is add water. I'm personally convinced that it tastes best when it has rained all night and your feet are freezing, and you all look like something the cat dragged home — but don't take my word for it, give it a try!*

5 cups	flour	1.25 L
½ cup	lard	125 mL
1 tsp.	salt	5 mL
2 tbsp.	baking powder	30 mL
¼ cup	oil (approximately)	60 mL

At Home:

1. Mix all the ingredients together, except the oil, cutting the lard in with a pastry blender until finely blended. Store in an airtight container.

On The Trail:

1. Heat the oil in a frying pan over an open fire or camp stove.
2. Mix 2 cups (500 mL) of bannock mix with 1 cup (250 mL) water.
3. Remove frying pan from heat and carefully pat bannock mixture into the pan.
4. Return pan to heat and fry bannock until it is golden brown around the edges. Flip bannock and fry until it is brown on the other side — about 10-15 minutes in total.

Serves: For 4 people, use 2 cups (500 mL) mix: 1 cup (250 mL) water. The recipe can be enlarged by keeping the same proportions.

* *See story, The Chilly Awakening, on page 50.*

See photograph on page 69.

Bannock On A Stick

This bannock can be mixed and squeezed onto one end of a stick in small amounts (so that the stick looks like a cattail). It can then be baked carefully by holding the stick over an open fire. The stick should be turned frequently and kept far enough from the fire to prevent the bannock from burning. When nicely browned, (about 15 minutes) break it off the stick and eat it with butter and jam. Yum!

Big Trout –

A 34-pound lake trout – a regular occurrence at North Knife Lake Lodge.

Blueberry or Cranberry Muffins

We only make these with berries that we have picked ourselves and there is no denying that wild berries have a superior flavor. But we can't be too "picky" in the off-season. A good blueberry muffin is hard to beat at any time.

1¾ cups	flour	425 mL
3½ tsp.	baking powder	17 mL
½ tsp.	salt	2 mL
¼ cup	white sugar	60 mL
1	egg	1
1¼ cups	milk	300 mL
¼ cup	vegetable oil	60 mL
¾ cup	blueberries OR cranberries	175 mL

1. In a large mixing bowl, combine flour, baking powder, salt and sugar.
2. Beat eggs, milk and oil together and add to dry ingredients. Stir only until mixture is moist. Batter will be lumpy.
3. Fold fresh blueberries or cranberries into the batter.
4. Fill WELL-GREASED muffin cups ⅔ full. Bake at 400°F (200°C) for 20-25 minutes, or until golden brown. Remove muffins from pans and serve warm or let cool.

Makes 12 large muffins.

VARIATION: If cultivated cranberries are being used, chop them first before adding to the batter or follow directions on package to make cranberry sauce. For Cranberry Sauce Muffins, reduce milk in muffin recipe to 1 cup (250 mL), and fold ½ cup (125 mL) cranberry sauce into batter.

See photograph on page 51.

Bran Muffin Mix

Since we first started using this bran muffin recipe, we've never looked back. There is only one word that aptly describes them — MOIST!

2 cups	boiling water	500 mL
2 cups	pure bran	500 mL
1 cup	butter OR margarine	250 mL
1 cup	white sugar	250 mL
3	eggs	3
4 cups	buttermilk*	1 L
5 cups	flour	1.25 L
3 tbsp.	baking soda	45 mL
1 tbsp.	salt	15 mL
4 cups	bran flakes	1 L
3½ cups	raisins	875 mL

 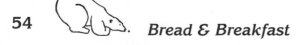

Bran Muffin Mix

Continued

1. Pour boiling water over bran and let stand for 5 minutes.
2. Cream butter and sugar. Add eggs, soaked bran and buttermilk. Add remaining ingredients and mix gently until moist.
3. Store batter in a large, airtight container; a 4-quart (4 L) ice-cream pail is perfect. Keep batter refrigerated and do not use for 24 hours after mixing. Batter will keep in the refrigerator for 6 weeks. Bake as needed.
4. To bake, fill greased muffin cups ¾ full. Bake at 400°F (200°C) for 15-20 minutes.

Makes 5 dozen muffins.

* *Buttermilk may be purchased in powdered form OR you may substitute sour milk. To make sour milk, add 1 tbsp. (15 mL) lemon juice or vinegar for each cup (250 mL) of milk.*

Marie's Mom's Yorkshire Pudding

We included this recipe because it is such a hard one to find and it is so good.

4	eggs	4
1 cup	flour	250 mL
1 cup	milk	250 mL
½ tsp.	salt	2 mL
	oil	

1. Beat eggs, flour, milk and salt well with a wire whisk or hand beater. Let the batter sit on the counter for 1-4 hours – it must be at room temperature. Beat the batter again, just before using.
2. About 20 minutes before serving, put 1 tsp. (5 mL) oil in each of 12 muffin cups and heat in a 450°F (230°C) oven until oil is hot, about 2 minutes.
3. Remove the pan from the oven and divide the batter between the cups. Cups will be about half full. Return the pan to the oven and bake for 15 minutes.
4. Turn Yorkshires out of muffin cups and serve immediately.

Makes 12.

COOKING TIP: Yorkshires will rise high and be well browned when done. BUT they will sink when removed from oven. This is normal!

My Mom also used to make this in a round, Pyrex casserole. To serve, she cut it in wedges, like a pie. That method makes a much denser and heavier Yorkshire, but I'm sure that's how it was done originally.

French Breakfast Muffins

Close your eyes, you'll think you're eating a cake doughnut. Sound tempting?

1½ cups+2 tbsp.	flour	400 mL
¾ cup	white sugar	175 mL
2 tsp.	baking powder	10 mL
¼ tsp.	salt	1 mL
¼ tsp.	nutmeg	1 mL
½ cup	milk	125 mL
1	egg, beaten	1
⅓ cup	butter OR margarine, melted	75 mL
3 tbsp.	butter, melted	45 mL
1 tsp.	cinnamon	5 mL
¼ cup	white sugar	60 mL
¼ tsp.	vanilla extract	1 mL

1. Combine flour, ¾ cup (175 mL) sugar, baking powder, salt and nutmeg. Add milk, egg and ⅓ cup (75 mL) melted butter. Mix thoroughly.
2. Grease 18 small muffin tins. Fill ½ full and bake at 400°F (200°C) for 20 minutes.
3. Remove muffins from the pan immediately. While warm, dip tops of muffins in the 3 tbsp. (45 mL) melted butter and roll in a mixture of the cinnamon, ¼ cup (60 mL) sugar and vanilla. Serve warm.

Makes 18 small muffins.

See photograph on page 51.

Blender Waffles

This is the only recipe I have found that does not require you to separate the egg yolks and egg whites and yet produces a superior waffle.

2 cups	flour	500 mL
½ tsp.	salt	2 mL
2 tsp.	baking powder	10 mL
1 tsp.	baking soda	5 mL
2 tbsp.	white sugar	30 mL
1 cup	sour cream	250 mL
1 cup	buttermilk OR sour milk	250 mL
3	eggs	3
½ cup	vegetable oil	125 mL

Blender Waffles

Continued

1. In a bowl, stir together flour, salt, baking powder, baking soda and sugar
2. Pour sour cream, buttermilk, eggs and oil into a blender and blend at high speed for 20 seconds. A hand blender works just as well.
3. Add dry ingredients to the blender and blend at medium speed for 1 minute. Stop blender and scrape sides, if necessary, during blending.
4. Grease and preheat a waffle iron, following the instructions that come with your iron. Place a heaping cup (250 mL plus) of batter on a 4-square waffle iron (a heaping ½ cup (125 mL plus) on a 2-square iron) and close the iron. Bake until golden brown on both sides.

Makes 4, 4-square waffles.

SERVING SUGGESTION: Serve with fresh, sweetened strawberries or Blueberry Sauce, page 198, and whipped cream or sour cream.

Apple Pancakes

A little bit of sweet for your breakfast, great for brunch, at home we even serve this for dinner when the "cook" gets lazy!

3 tbsp.	butter OR margarine	45 mL
4	apples, pared and sliced	4
¼ cup	sugar, brown OR white	60 mL
1 tsp.	cinnamon	5 mL
1 cup	milk	250 mL
6	eggs	6
1 cup	flour	250 mL
2 tsp.	white sugar	10 mL
½ tsp.	salt	2 mL

1. In a 10" (25 cm), ovenproof pan, melt butter. Add apples, sugar and cinnamon and cook on the top of the stove until the apples are soft, about 5 minutes. Taste for sweetness.
2. Meanwhile, mix milk, eggs, flour, sugar and salt, beating well.
3. Pour the batter over the cooked apples. You may want to sprinkle some sugar and cinnamon over the batter for added flavor.
4. Bake, UNCOVERED, in a 425°F (220°C) oven for 20-25 minutes.

Serves 4.

SERVING SUGGESTIONS: Cut the pancake in wedges and serve from the pan. Serve with maple syrup, sour cream or ice cream. This is also good on its own.

NOTE: For a thinner pancake, halve the ingredients for the batter but bake in the same-size pan. Reduce baking time by 5 minutes.

Sour Cream Pancakes

This recipe has evolved at our house over the years and has spread far and wide. We have served these to people from all around the world and they always have seconds. They are great served with maple syrup or heaped with sweetened strawberries and piled high with whipped cream. Add fresh blueberries to the batter or serve them with Blueberry Sauce, page 198.

2 cups	flour	500 mL
2 tsp.	baking powder	10 mL
1 tsp.	baking soda	5 mL
2 tsp.	sugar	10 mL
½ tsp.	salt	2 mL
2	eggs, slightly beaten	2
½ cup	sour cream	125 mL
2 cups	milk	500 mL

1. In a large mixing bowl, mix together the flour, baking powder, baking soda, sugar and salt.
2. In a separate bowl, mix the eggs, sour cream and milk. Beat well with a wire whisk.
3. Pour the milk mixture into the dry ingredients and beat with the wire whisk until the batter is fairly smooth. A few small lumps won't hurt the pancakes.
4. Heat a greased griddle or heavy frying pan over medium-high heat. Pour batter onto the hot griddle and cook until the top is bubbly and the pancake is slightly dry around the edges. Turn and cook on the other side until just golden brown.

Makes about 16, 5" (13 cm) pancakes.

NOTE: Now, I have to tell you that pancake preferences are kind of a personal thing. We like ours on the thinner, lighter side so I often add just a little more milk. With a little practice you can make them to your own liking.

See photograph on page 51.

Overnight Cheese Strata

This is a regular Sunday morning breakfast for us in September at the hunting lodge. It makes our morning just a bit more relaxed, since the work is done the night before. Until 1993, hunting was illegal on Sundays in Manitoba, and everybody got to sleep in. But now the alarm clock goes off at 4 a.m. just like any other day. I wonder how the hunters would feel about a "Do It Yourself Day"?

6 cups	bread cut in 1/2" (1.3 cm) cubes	1.5 L
2 cups	shredded medium OR sharp Cheddar cheese	500 mL
1 lb.	bacon, cooked and crumbled, OR chopped ham	500 g
1/4 cup	chopped green pepper	60 mL
6	large eggs	6
4 cups	whole milk	1 L
1 tsp.	dry mustard	5 mL
1/2 tsp.	salt	2 mL
1/4 tsp.	pepper	1 mL
1/4 cup	chopped green onion	60 mL
1/2 cup	butter OR margarine, melted	125 mL

1. Place half the bread cubes in the bottom of a greased 9 x 13" (23 x 33 cm) pan. Scatter the cheese, bacon and green pepper over the bread. Cover with the remainder of the bread cubes.
2. Beat the eggs with the milk, dry mustard, salt and pepper. Pour evenly over the bread cubes. Refrigerate overnight.
3. Before baking, sprinkle with green onions; drizzle with melted butter.
4. Set the pan in a pan of hot water. Bake, uncovered, at 300°F (150°C) for 1 1/2 hours.

Serves 12.

SERVING SUGGESTION: We like to serve this with Blueberry or Cranberry Muffins, page 54, or warm Cinnamon Buns, page 39.

Blessed are Thou, O Lord our God, King of the universe, who has kept us in life and sustained us and enabled us to reach this season.

Rabbi Hayim Halevy Donin

Eggs Benedict

When we serve Eggs Benedict at the Lodges, it takes a production line in the kitchen. But it can be simple, yet elegant to serve at home, with our Easy Blender Hollandaise Sauce.

> **English muffins, purchased OR as page 37,**
>   **split and toasted**
> **ham OR back bacon, sliced and cooked**
> **poached eggs**
> **Hollandaise sauce, below**

1. On each plate, lay 1 or 2 halves of toasted English Muffins.
2. Top each half with a piece of warm ham or bacon.
3. Place a poached egg on top of the meat.
4. Ladle about 2 tbsp. (30 mL) of Hollandaise sauce over each egg.

Easy Blender Hollandaise Sauce

3	egg yolks	3
1 tbsp.	lemon juice	15 mL
dash	cayenne pepper OR paprika	dash
¾ cup	butter, melted	175 mL

1. Blend egg yolks, lemon juice and cayenne in a blender.
2. Add hot, melted butter SLOWLY, while blending. This is important to the success of your sauce. If butter is added too quickly, the yolk does not absorb the butter and does not thicken properly.
3. This sauce will keep warm in a covered blender for 15-20 minutes.

Makes 1 cup (250 mL) of sauce.

HELPFUL HINT: Don't try to warm the sauce in your microwave — unless you want scrambled eggs!

To reheat the sauce, warm it carefully over low heat in a saucepan or in a double boiler, stirring constantly.

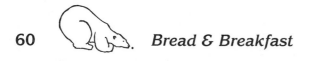

Midday Madness

Lunches & Soups

What shall we have for lunch? This is one of the questions we ask each other most frequently at the lodge. The fishermen are usually out for a shore lunch, but every once in a while, if the rain drives them in, we have to make lunch. Our hunters at Dymond Lake are a different story. Some of them take their lunches and some of them come in every day. In fact, some of them take their lunches and have it eaten by nine o'clock so they come in for lunch too. That is why we pride ourselves on being very inventive when it comes to our hearty homemade soups — they sometimes have to really stretch. We do have a few good, hearty lunch standbys that always seem to be a hit. Don't limit them to lunches though, we often serve them for dinner at home.

Pizza Buns

This was a great lunch favorite for both the Woolsey and the Webber kids when they were growing up. Now we team it up with one of our hearty soups for a lunch fit for any fisherman, fisherwoman or fisherchild! It is very simple and you usually have enough ingredients on hand to come up with these on short notice.

½ cup	finely chopped pepperoni	125 mL
¼ cup	finely chopped green pepper	60 mL
¼ cup	finely chopped onion	60 mL
¼ cup	finely chopped mushrooms (fresh OR canned)	60 mL
½ cup	grated cheese (mozzarella, Cheddar OR a combination)	125 mL
⅓ cup	ketchup	75 mL
1 tsp.	leaf oregano	5 mL
1 tsp.	DLS* (if you do not have DLS add 1 tsp. [5 mL] basil leaves and salt and pepper to taste) dinner buns	5 mL

1. In a medium-sized bowl, combine all of the ingredients except the buns.
2. Halve dinner rolls and spread each half with 2 tbsp. (30 mL) of filling.
2. Place the pizza buns on a baking tray and bake in a 350°F (180°C) oven for 8-10 minutes, or until buns are hot and cheese is melted.

Makes enough filling for 20 bun halves.

VARIATION: This is also very good if you spread it on a loaf of French Bread, sliced lengthwise. Increase the baking time to 20 minutes. Slice thickly to serve

* *Dymond Lake Seasoning*

Fried Bread

An easy way to dress up ordinary bread and make lunch a little more special.

> **bread**
> **butter**
> **Dymond Lake Seasoning***

1. If you are slicing the bread yourself, slice it thick! Butter both sides of bread. Sprinkle both sides with Dymond Lake Seasoning*. Fry on both sides until browned. Serve hot.

* *Try this with garlic salt or your favorite seasoning.*

Pizza Pizza Pizza

This, as you can probably guess, is a real hit with the guests and the staff. In fact, every once in a while we have a pizza and games night for the staff and guests. Our greatest challenge in the kitchen is making one of the pizzas hot enough to make our pilot, Jerzy, yell "Uncle". Read on for some of our combinations.

Pizza Dough

2¼ cups	warm water	550 mL
¼ cup	oil	60 mL
2 tsp.	salt	10 mL
5½ cups	flour	1.4 L
2 tbsp.	instant yeast*	30 mL

1. Measure the warm water into a large bowl (into your mixer bowl if you are fortunate enough to have a dough hook).
2. Add the oil, salt, 2 cups (500 mL) of flour and the yeast. Beat the batter with an electric beater or a wire whisk for about 2 minutes.
3. Switch to a dough hook, if you have one, and add the rest of the flour, gradually. Knead until dough isn't too sticky to handle. If kneading by hand, add as much flour as you can in the bowl, then turn out dough onto a FLOURED surface, and work in the rest of the flour by hand, using a kneading motion. Knead for about 5 minutes. It may take MORE or LESS flour.
4. Place the dough in a greased bowl and cover with a clean cloth*, put in a warm spot and let it rise for 10-15 minutes while you mix up the Pizza Sauce, page 64.
5. Divide the dough into 3 equal pieces and with greased hands push and spread the dough to cover the greased pizza pans.

This makes enough dough for 3 pizzas.

NOTE: The nice thing about the recipe is that if you don't need to make 3 pizzas. Just seal the extra dough in a zip-lock bag and freeze it until the next time you want to make pizza. OR make 3 pizzas and freeze the ones you don't need. To reheat, place frozen pizza in a 350°F (180°C) oven for 30 minutes. Extra Pizza Sauce may be frozen as well.

* See notes on YEAST and RISING TECHNIQUES on page 36.

Pizza Sauce & Toppings

This is a pizza sauce that we have developed and perfected over the years. If it is not spicy enough for you just go ahead and experiment. We use our homemade spaghetti sauce too, page 144, and we are not above buying our favorite commercial pizza sauce and using that instead.

5½ oz.	can tomato paste	156 mL
1 tsp.	dried sweet basil	5 mL
½ tsp.	dried oregano	2 mL
1	garlic clove, minced OR ½ tsp. (2 mL) garlic powder	1
½ tsp.	DLS* OR ¼ tsp. (1 mL) salt & ½ tsp. (2 mL) seasoned pepper	2 mL

Toppings:

sliced pepperoni
cooked hamburger
sliced ham
pineapple tidbits
chopped onions
chopped green peppers
sliced green olives
sliced black olives
sliced mushrooms
chopped jalapeños
crushed dried chili peppers

3 cups	shredded mozzarella	750 mL
3 cups	shredded Cheddar cheese	750 mL

1. In a small bowl, mix the pizza sauce ingredients well, divide evenly and spread over the 3 pizza crusts.
2. Top with any combination of the toppings.
3. Sprinkle each pizza with cheeses.
4. Bake at 375°F (190°C) for 18-20 minutes.

* *Dymond Lake Seasoning*

"Jerzy's Special Pizza Topping"

cooked hamburger
sliced pepperoni
chopped onion
chopped green pepper
sliced mushrooms

2 tbsp.	chopped jalapeños OR more	30 mL
1 tbsp.	dried chili peppers	
15 mL		

Taco Salad

A meal in itself, and one that is easy to serve to a family. The guides and staff at North Knife Lake give their hearty approval to this winning lunch.

1 lb.	hamburger	500 g
4	green onions, chopped	4
2 tbsp.	soy sauce	30 mL
1 oz.	pkg. Taco Seasoning	35 g
1 tbsp.	chili powder	15 mL
14 oz.	can tomato sauce	398 mL
1 tbsp.	DLS *	15 mL
1	small head of lettuce, chopped	1
2	large tomatoes, chopped	2
1 cup	grated medium Cheddar cheese	250 mL
1 cup	Ranch Dressing	250 mL
12½ oz.	pkg. Taco OR nacho chips, broken	350 g

1. Brown the hamburger with the green onions. Drain off fat. Add the soy sauce, Taco Seasoning, chili powder, tomato sauce and DLS*. Simmer 20 minutes. You may let the meat cool or continue with the hot meat mixture.
2. Toss the meat mixture with lettuce, tomatoes, cheese and dressing. Add the chips, toss again, and serve immediately.

Serves 4.

SERVING SUGGESTION: Taco Salad may be served while the meat is still warm or after it has cooled.

* *Dymond Lake Seasoning makes the salad a little hotter and spicier. It will still taste fine without it, but you may wish to add extra pepper.*

> **The man on the bridge addressed the solitary fisherman.**
>
> **"Any luck?" he asked.**
>
> **"Any luck!" was the answer. "Why, I got forty pike out of here yesterday."**
>
> **"Do you know who I am?"**
>
> **"No," said the fisherman.**
>
> **"I'm the chief magistrate here, and all this estate is mine."**
>
> **"And do you know who I am?" asked the fisherman, quickly.**
>
> **"No."**
>
> **"I'm the biggest liar in Virginia."**

Hamburger Noodle Bake

This is another of those great recipes that freezes so well. So, why not make two and get one into the freezer.

8 oz.	pkg. medium egg noodles	250 g
2 lbs.	hamburger	1 kg
1 tbsp.	DLS* OR 1 tsp. (5 mL) seasoned salt and 1 tsp. (5 mL) seasoned pepper	15 mL
1 tsp.	salt	5 mL
2 tsp.	sugar	10 mL
2	garlic cloves, crushed	2
2 x 14 oz.	cans tomato sauce	2 x 398 mL
4 oz.	cream cheese, at room temperature	125 g
1 cup	sour cream	250 mL
6	small green onions, chopped	6
1½ cups	grated medium Cheddar cheese	375 mL

1. Cook the noodles according to package directions.
2. Brown the hamburger, drain off fat and add spices, sugar, garlic and tomato sauce. Simmer for 10 minutes to blend flavors.
3. Cream the cheese and add sour cream and onions.
4. Place half of the noodles in the bottom of a 4-quart (4 L) casserole or 9 x 13" (23 x 33 cm) baking dish. Cover with half of the cheese mixture and then half of the meat mixture. Repeat. Top with the grated cheese.
4. Bake, uncovered, at 350°F (180°C) for 30-40 minutes, until hot and bubbly and the cheese is melted.

Serves 6.

VARIATION: An equal amount of creamed cottage cheese can be substituted for the cream cheese and sour cream, if you like.

**God bless this bunch
As we munch our lunch.**

Midday Madness

Sausage Combo

This is another of the infamous Len's recipes. It doubles and triples very well so think of this the next time you are hosting a big football or hockey windup party! Throw together a nice tossed salad and pull out some piping hot Crusty French Bread and you'll rate as "Most Valuable Player".

8	slices bacon, diced in 1" (2.5 cm) pieces	8
1 lb.	beef sausage, cut in 1" (2.5 cm) pieces	500 g
1½ tsp.	reserved drippings	7 mL
⅔ cup	sliced celery	150 mL
1 cup	chopped onion	250 mL
⅔ cup	chopped green pepper	150 mL
14 oz.	can kidney beans	398 mL
14 oz.	can pork and beans	398 mL
1	garlic clove, crushed	1
1	large tomato, chopped	1
2 tsp.	Worcestershire sauce	10 mL
½ tsp.	dry mustard	2 mL
1½ cups	grated medium Cheddar cheese	375 mL

1. In a skillet, sauté bacon and sausage until browned. Remove from the pan and set aside.
2. In the reserved drippings, sauté celery, onion and green pepper.
3. Combine sausage, bacon, vegetables, kidney beans, pork and beans, garlic, tomato, Worcestershire and the dry mustard in a 3-quart (3 L) casserole or Dutch oven.
4. Bake, covered, in a 375°F (190°C) oven for 30 minutes. Remove from the oven and sprinkle with the cheese. Return to the oven and continue to bake, uncovered, for another 15 minutes.

Serves 4-6.

NOTE: This freezes well!

Sloppy Joes — Something's Fishy Here!

This is not your traditional Sloppy Joe with lots of tomato sauce, but keep an open mind. I am sure that you will find them a pleasant surprise for a quick lunch. Good enough for company!

4 oz.	can tuna	115 g
¾ cup	mayonnaise	175 mL
1 cup	grated Cheddar cheese	250 mL
2 tbsp.	finely chopped green pepper	30 mL
2 tbsp.	finely chopped green olives	30 mL
2 tbsp.	finely chopped onion	30 mL
3	hard-boiled eggs, chopped	3
10	buns	10

1. Mix all ingredients, except the buns, in a bowl.
2. Spread filling on split buns; place on an ungreased baking sheet.
3. Broil just until golden brown and bubbly. You can also just bake them in a 375°F (190°C) oven for 8-10 minutes.

The filling makes enough for 20 bun halves.

VARIATION: These are just as good with chopped ham instead of tuna!

"While fishing one day," said the old-timer, "I ran short of bait and was temporarily at a loss as to what to do. Near my feet, I noticed a small snake which held a frog in its mouth. I removed the frog and cut it up for bait, feeling very fortunate that my eyes had lighted on the snake at that moment.

"I did, however, feel a bit guilty at relieving the poor reptile of his meal and in order to give him a slight recompense for my supply of bait, I poured a few drops of whisky into its mouth. Fortunately for my conscience, the snake seemed to leave in a contented mood, and I turned and went on fishing.

"Some time had passed when I felt something hitting against the leg of my boot. Looking down, I saw the identical snake, laden with three more frogs!"

Soup and Salad

Marie's Fish Chowder, page 28
Pepper and Sugar Pea Salad, page 119
Camping Bannock, page 53

Cream of Wild Rice Soup

When you are served this at one of the Lodges, you have probably had Marie's Wild Rice Casserole Suprême, page 126, for dinner the night before. It is very good made with leftover casserole, but just as good made from scratch.

4 cups	cooked wild rice (1 cup [250 mL] uncooked)	1 L
1	large onion, diced	1
½	green pepper, diced	½
2	celery ribs, diced	2
½ cup	butter OR margarine	125 mL
1 cup	flour	250 mL
8 cups	hot chicken broth	2 L
10 oz.	can mushrooms, drained	284 mL
	salt and pepper and DLS* OR a pinch of thyme and basil, to taste	
1 cup	light cream OR canned milk	250 mL

1. Prepare the rice if you are not using leftovers.
2. Sauté onions, green pepper and celery in butter until vegetables are soft, about 5 minutes.
3. Stir in flour.
4. Gradually add hot chicken broth, stirring to blend well.
5. Add mushrooms, cooked rice and seasonings. Heat to boiling.
6. Add cream and reheat before serving. DO NOT BOIL once cream has been added.

Serves 8-10.

* *Dymond Lake Seasoning*

> *While a shooting party was out for a day's sport a raw young hunter was observed taking aim at a pheasant running along the ground. As it is unsportsmanlike to shoot a bird while it is on the ground, a companion shouted: "Hey, there, never shoot a running bird!"*
>
> *"What do you take me for, you idiot?" came the reply. "Can't you see I'm waiting till it stops?"*

Lake Pike –

"It doesn't get much better than this!"

Dymond Lake Leftovers Soup

DAY 1: Have Jalapeño Goose with Wild Rice and Mushroom Casserole, for dinner.

DAY 2: Have Cream of Wild Rice Soup made with the leftover Wild Rice Casserole for lunch and cook a turkey dinner with all the trimmings.

DAY 3: Make Turkey Soup for lunch from last night's leftover mashed potatoes, stuffing, carrots, gravy and turkey; prepare Mushroom Goose for dinner.

DAY 4: Combine the leftover Turkey Soup with the leftover Cream of Wild Rice Soup with the leftover Mushroom Goose and some frozen leftover white rice that was left over from the Goose Gumbo one day last week.

Days 1 through 3 are fairly normal. But once, on Day 4, we got caught short by hunters who ate their packed lunches at 10:00 a.m., and arrived at noon for a hot lunch at the Lodge. Undaunted, we presented them with this delightful combination. Nor were we surprised when one of them asked for the recipe. That's an everyday occurrence at the lodges. But this one couldn't be duplicated. It was truly an original!

Jeanne's Croûtons

A tasty way to spice up your soup or salad.

1 tsp.	dried dillweed	5 mL
1	small garlic clove, crushed OR ½ tsp. (2 mL) garlic powder	1
½ tsp.	seasoned pepper	2 mL
2 tbsp.	DLS*	30 mL
⅓ cup	olive oil	75 mL
1	loaf day-old bread, cubed	1

1. Mix dillweed, garlic, seasoned pepper, DLS* and olive oil in a bowl.
2. Add the bread cubes all at once and mix well.
3. Spread on a baking sheet and bake at 300°F (150°C) for 50-60 minutes, or until lightly browned and crisp.

Makes 8 cups (2 L) of Croûtons.

NOTE: Just bag or freeze any leftover croûtons and you will have them ready for your next Caesar salad. Or float a few croûtons on top of your homemade soup.

* For Dymond Lake Seasoning substitute 1 tsp. (5 mL) seasoned salt, ½ tsp. (2 mL) each of onion powder, oregano, basil, parsley and thyme. Increase seasoned pepper to 2 tsp. (10 mL).

Tomato Chicken Rice Soup

(MARIE) *This chicken soup is not made from leftovers or from bones and skin. This time we're using whole, fresh chicken parts. I choose to use breasts only, but legs would be just as good. A personal favorite!*

1	whole chicken breast (2 halves)	1
6 cups	water	1.5 L
1	medium onion, chopped	1
2	celery ribs, chopped	2
1	carrot, chopped	1
½	green pepper, chopped	½
1	garlic clove, crushed	1
2 tbsp.	olive oil OR butter OR margarine	30 mL
2 tbsp.	chicken bouillon	30 mL
¼ cup	raw rice	60 mL
½ tsp.	seasoned pepper	2 mL
28 oz.	can tomatoes, blended	796 mL

1. In a large saucepan, combine chicken breasts and water. Bring to a boil and simmer for ½-1 hour, until tender. Reserving the broth for step 3, remove the chicken and let it cool. Cut into bite-sized pieces.
2. In another pan, over medium heat, sauté onion, celery, carrot, green pepper and garlic in olive oil until onions are transparent and carrots are almost tender, about 10 minutes.
3. To the chicken broth, add the sautéed vegetables, bouillon, rice and pepper. Bring to a boil and simmer for 20 minutes, or until the rice is tender.
4. Add the tomatoes and the chicken. Add salt and more pepper, if desired.
5. Reheat and serve.

Serves 4-6.

Mmmmmm! My mouth waters just thinking about it.

*There are two time periods when fishing is good —
before you get there and after you leave.*

Turkey Carcass Soup

This is a recipe that almost didn't make it into the book because we just assumed that all "old" cooks would know how to do it. SO . . . this is for all you "young" cooks who want to be "old" cooks someday.

Day 1:
1. Roast a turkey with dressing, see page 161, and serve it with mashed potatoes, carrots and gravy. Save all the bones and skin.
2. Place the bones and skin in a large Dutch oven, or use the roasting pan that you just made gravy in. (Don't even wash it!) Refrigerate it until tomorrow because you're too tired to make soup tonight. OR freeze it until you are ready to make soup.

Day 2:
1. Cover the bones with water. Add **1 tsp. (5 mL) salt, ½ tsp. (2 mL) seasoned pepper, a bay leaf and 1 tbsp. (15 mL) DLS***. Bring to a boil and simmer for 1-2 hours. Strain out all the bones and skin. Remove any turkey from the bones and set it aside. Discard the bones, skin, and bay leaf.
2. At this point, you may wish to let the broth cool. When it does, any fat that it contains will rise to the surface and congeal, so that you can scrape it off and dispose of it.
   OR You may simply continue. The soup will not taste greasy!
3. To the broth, add:

1	**onion, chopped**	1
	a few ribs of celery with leaves, chopped	
2	**carrots, chopped, if you didn't have enough leftovers**	2

   Simmer for 20 minutes, or until vegetables are soft.
4. Add the **leftover mashed potatoes (broken into small chunks), the leftover carrots chopped up, the dressing and the gravy****. Reheat, adjust seasonings and serve.

* *If you don't use Dymond Lake Seasoning, you'll want to use more salt and pepper. If you didn't have much dressing left over to add to the soup, you may want to add some sage or poultry seasoning.*

** *Other leftover vegetables may also be added, like broccoli, corn, beans, peas. Be creative.*

Hamburger Soup

A family favorite. It sticks to your ribs and kids love it!

1½ lbs.	ground beef	750 g
1	medium onion, chopped	1
28 oz.	can tomatoes, chopped	796 mL
6 cups	beef broth	1.5 L
4	carrots, chopped	4
4	celery ribs, chopped	4
½	green pepper, chopped	½
½ cup	pot barley	125 mL
2 tbsp.	parsley	30 mL
1 tbsp.	DLS*	15 mL

1. Brown meat and onions. Drain well.
2. Combine all ingredients in a large pot. Bring to a boil. Simmer, covered, for at least 2 hours to make sure the barley is cooked.
3. Taste to adjust seasonings.

Makes at least 10 servings and freezes well.

* *For Dymond Lake Seasoning substitute ½ tsp. (2 mL) thyme, ¼ tsp. (1 mL) pepper, ½ tsp. (2 mL) celery salt, ¼ tsp. (1 mL) garlic powder.*

Be present at our table Lord
With guests we must but can't afford!
And let there be no strain or fuss
As if we always feasted thus.
And let the daily woman stay
Till half past two to clear away.

Minestrone

(MARIE) I confess that I am a lover of good, homemade soup. I think I should have been a pioneer. This is a meal in itself. Serve with hot buns, tea biscuits or bannock.

½ lb.	ground pork OR beef	250 g
2 tbsp.	olive oil OR cooking oil	30 mL
1	large onion, chopped	1
2	garlic cloves, minced	2
½ cup	chopped celery	125 mL
½ cup	chopped carrots	125 mL
½ cup	chopped green pepper	125 mL
2 tbsp.	chopped parsley	30 mL
½ tsp.	dried basil	2 mL
¼ tsp.	dried thyme	1 mL
1	bay leaf	1
½ tsp.	salt	2 mL
	pepper OR DLS* to taste	
19 oz.	can tomatoes, chopped	540 mL
4 cups	chicken broth	1 L
2 cups	shredded cabbage	500 mL
14 oz.	can kidney beans	398 mL
½ cup	elbow macaroni OR other pasta, uncooked	125 mL

1. In a large, heavy saucepan, brown the ground meat slightly to remove the fat. Strain off the fat and discard. Return meat to saucepan.
2. Add olive oil, onion, garlic, celery, carrots, green pepper and seasonings. Cook over medium heat until vegetables are softened, about 10 minutes.
3. Add the rest of the ingredients. Bring to a boil and simmer for 30 minutes. If too thick, dilute with water to desired consistency.
4. Taste and adjust seasonings.

Serves 6-8.

* *Dymond Lake Seasoning*

*Come, Lord Jesus, be our guest,
And may our meal by you be blest.
Martin Luther (1483 — 1546)*

Cream of Broccoli or Cauliflower Soup

A good, basic recipe for cream of anything soup! Experiment with whatever left-overs you have, and savor the results!

Base:

¼ cup	chopped onion	60 mL
¼ cup	chopped celery	60 mL
¼ cup	butter OR margarine	60 mL
3 tbsp.	flour	45 mL
1 tsp.	DLS* OR a few mixed herbs and ¼ tsp. (1 mL) pepper	5 mL
1½ cups	chicken broth	375 mL
1½ cups	light cream OR canned milk	375 mL

Broccoli Soup:

2 cups	cooked, chopped broccoli	500 mL
1 tbsp.	coarsely chopped fresh parsley OR 1 tsp. (5 mL) dried	15 mL

Cauliflower Soup:

2 cups	cooked, chopped cauliflower	500 mL
½ tsp.	dillweed	2 mL
1 tbsp.	coarsely chopped fresh parsley OR 1 tsp. (5 mL) dried	15 mL

1. Sauté onion and celery in butter until tender.
2. Stir in flour and DLS*, and cook for 1 minute, stirring constantly.
3. Add chicken broth and milk, stirring until thickened.
4. Add one of the vegetable mixtures to the cream base and heat gently. DO NOT BOIL once the milk has been added.

Serves 4-6.

* *Dymond Lake Seasoning*

PARSON "Do you know the parables, my child?"
JOHNNY "Yes, sir."
PARSON "And which one of the parables do you like best?"
JOHNNY "I like the one where somebody loafs and fishes."

Cream of Potato Soup

Make this soup from scratch or make it from leftover potatoes. Use it as a meal starter or as a lunch on its own. The condiments really dress this up. Use your favorite or choose them all. Ummmmm, good!

Soup:

1	medium onion, chopped	1
¼ cup	butter OR margarine	60 mL
4 cups	potatoes, peeled and diced	1 L
3 cups	chicken broth	750 mL
½ cup	canned milk OR light cream	125 mL
1 tsp.	DLS* OR ½ tsp. (2 mL) seasoned pepper and	5 mL
	½ tsp. (2 mL) celery salt	
	salt and pepper to taste	

Condiments:

crisp seasoned croûtons
crumbled bacon
chopped fresh parsley
chopped green onions

1. In a large saucepan, cook the onion in the butter until the onion is soft, about 5 minutes.
2. Add the potatoes and chicken broth Bring to a boil and simmer 30-40 minutes, until the potatoes are very soft.
3. Put the soup in a blender and make a purée**. (You will want to do this in 2 or 3 installments.)
4. Return the purée to the saucepan. Add milk. Reheat, taste and add DLS* salt and pepper to taste.

Serves 4.

SERVING SUGGESTIONS: Serve with separate bowls of croûtons, bacon, fresh parsley and chopped green onions. Try Jeanne's Croûtons, page 72.

* *Dymond Lake Seasoning.*
** *PURÉE: A thick liquid suspension made from finely ground or mashed food.*

Stop and Snack Awhile

This section is full of good snackin' numbers. We use the cookies for shore lunches at North Knife and bag lunches at Dymond Lake. These treats provide the tantalizing smells that emanate daily from the kitchens. With a large number of guests and staff to feed we always like to have lots of snacks on hand. But they are especially appreciated when unexpected guests drop in from the sky — not an unusual occurrence at either of the Lodges.

P.S. During one hunting season at Dymond Lake (which is only three weeks), Doug's Mother kept track and she made in excess of 2000 cookies. That's a lot of dough!

Melt-In-Your-Mouth Chocolate Chip Cookies

It must be the cream of tartar that makes these melt in your mouth!

½ cup	butter OR margarine	125 mL
1 cup	shortening	250 mL
½ cup	white sugar	125 mL
½ cup	brown sugar	125 mL
1	egg	1
2¼ cups	flour	550 mL
1 tsp.	baking soda	5 mL
1 tsp.	cream of tartar	5 mL
⅛ tsp.	salt	0.5 mL
1 tsp.	vanilla	5 mL
1 cup	chocolate chips	250 mL

1. Cream together butter, shortening and sugars.
2. Add egg, then flour, baking soda, cream of tartar, salt and vanilla. Blend well.
3. Mix in chocolate chips.
4. Drop dough by tablespoonfuls (15 mL plus) onto an ungreased baking sheet.
5. Bake cookies in a 400°F (200°C) oven for 7-10 minutes.

Makes 2-3 dozen cookies and doubles well.

Soft Chocolate Cookies

A cake-like cookie that begs to be eaten fresh from the oven.

⅔ cup	butter OR margarine	150 mL
1 cup	white sugar	250 mL
1	egg	1
1 tsp.	vanilla	5 mL
½ cup	cocoa	125 mL
1¾ cups	flour	425 mL
½ tsp.	baking soda	2 mL
½ tsp.	salt	2 mL
½ cup	water	125 mL
1 cup	chocolate chips	250 mL

Stop and Snack Awhile

Soft Chocolate Cookies

Continued

1. Cream together the butter and sugar. Add egg and vanilla.
2. In a separate bowl, sift cocoa into flour, baking soda and salt and mix well.
3. Add dry ingredients to creamed mixture alternately with water, mixing well after each addition.
4. Add chocolate chips.
5. Drop dough by heaping tablespoonfuls (15 mL plus) onto an ungreased baking sheet. Bake at 350°F (180°C) for 8-10 minutes. The centers should still be a little soft. Remove cookies from the baking sheet immediately and cool on a rack.

Makes 2 dozen large cookies — if you can keep them long enough to count them!

Gourmet Chocolate Cookies

Some might call these double chocolate. They are firmer than our soft chocolate cookie and they travel well in lunches.

1¼ cups	butter OR margarine, softened	300 mL
1½ cups	sugar	375 mL
2	eggs	2
⅔ cup	cocoa	150 mL
2½ cups	flour	625 mL
2 tsp.	baking soda	10 mL
1 cup	chocolate chips	250 mL
½ cup	chopped nuts	125 mL

1. Cream together butter and sugar. Add eggs.
2. Sift cocoa into flour and baking soda. Add to creamed mixture.
3. Add chocolate chips and nuts.
4. Drop dough by heaping tablespoonfuls (15 mL plus) onto an ungreased baking sheet. Flatten dough slightly with your fingers.
5. Bake at 350°F (180°C) for 12-15 minutes. Let cookies cool for 5 minutes on the baking sheet before removing to a cooling rack.

Makes 2-3 dozen large cookies.

NOTE: This recipe doubles well.

See photograph on the back cover.

Chocolate Chip Crispy Cookies

At the camps, we experiment a lot with cookie recipes. A favorite of almost every-one is the chocolate chip cookie. But everyone has their own version of his/her favorite. We've chosen to share two with you — one plain, one with added crunch — both melt-in-your-mouth delicious.

1 cup	butter OR margarine	250 mL
1 cup	brown sugar	250 mL
1 cup	white sugar	250 mL
¾ cup	vegetable oil	175 mL
1	egg	1
1 tsp.	vanilla	5 mL
3½ cups	flour	875 mL
1 tsp.	salt	5 mL
1 tsp.	baking soda	5 mL
1 tsp.	cream of tartar	5 mL
1 cup	rolled oats	250 mL
1 cup	Rice Krispies	250 mL
1 cup	chocolate chips	250 mL

1. In a large mixing bowl, cream the butter and the sugars.
2. Add oil, egg and vanilla and mix well for at least 3 minutes.
3. Combine the flour, salt, baking soda and cream of tartar and add to the sugar mixture.
4. Mix in the oats, Rice Krispies and chocolate chips.
5. Roll heaping tablespoonfuls (15 mL plus) of dough into balls, a little smaller than a golf ball.
6. Place balls 2" (5 cm) apart on an ungreased cookie sheet. Press down with a fork.
7. Bake in a 350°F (180°C) oven for 12-15 minutes, until golden brown.
8. Allow cookies to cool slightly before removing from the baking sheet to a cooling rack.

Makes 5 dozen cookies.

VARIATION: Substitute Smarties and nuts for chocolate chips.

See photograph on the back cover.

 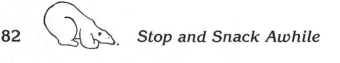

Gingersnaps

If it is a crackle-topped gingersnap you crave, this one has always worked for us!

¾ cups	margarine OR shortening	175 mL
1 cup	white sugar	250 mL
1	egg	1
¼ cup	molasses	60 mL
2 cups	flour	500 mL
1 tsp.	baking soda	5 mL
1 tsp.	cinnamon	5 mL
1 tsp.	cloves	5 mL
1 tsp.	ginger	5 mL
	white sugar	

1. Cream together margarine and sugar.
2. Beat in egg and molasses.
3. Mix flour, baking soda, cinnamon, cloves and ginger. Add to the creamed mixture.
4. Form heaping tablespoonfuls (15 mL plus) of dough into small balls, smaller than a golf ball.
5. Roll dough balls in sugar. Do not flatten.
6. Place balls 2" (5 cm) apart on an ungreased baking sheet and bake at 375°F (190°C) for 10 minutes, or until tops are crackled and lightly browned.
7. Let cookies cool 10 minutes on the baking sheet before removing them to a cooling rack.

Makes 2-3 dozen cookies.

NOTE: This recipe doubles well.

See photograph on the back cover.

A fisherman got such a reputation for stretching the truth that he bought a pair of scales and insisted on weighing every fish he caught, in the presence of a witness.

One day a doctor borrowed the fisherman's scales to weigh a new-born baby. The baby weighed forty-seven pounds.

Dad's Cookies

Yes, these taste like the real thing — dark, crisp and spicy.

1 cup	butter OR margarine	250 mL
1½ cups	white sugar	375 mL
2	eggs	2
2 tbsp.	corn syrup	30 mL
2 cups	flour	500 mL
½ tsp.	salt	2 mL
1 tbsp.	baking soda	15 mL
½ tsp.	allspice	2 mL
2 tsp.	cinnamon	10 mL
2 tsp.	ginger	10 mL
2 cups	rolled oats	500 mL
½ cup	unsweetened, desiccated coconut	125 mL

1. Cream together the butter and sugar. Add eggs and corn syrup and beat well.
2. Mix flour, salt, baking soda and spices with rolled oats and coconut. Add to creamed mixture.
3. Drop dough by heaping tablespoonfuls (15 mL plus) on a greased cookie sheet. Flatten with a fork dipped in flour. Bake at 350°F (180°C) for 12-15 minutes. Remove cookies to a cooling rack.

Makes 2-3 dozen cookies.

Peanut Butter Cookies

Some like them crunchy and some like them smooth. We make them both ways with equal approval.

1 cup	butter OR margarine	250 mL
1 cup	white sugar	250 mL
1 cup	brown sugar	250 mL
1 cup	peanut butter (crunchy OR smooth)	250 mL
2	eggs	2
1 tsp.	vanilla	5 mL
3 cups	flour	750 mL
2 tsp.	baking soda	10 mL
½ tsp.	salt	2 mL

  *Stop and Snack Awhile*

Peanut Butter Cookies

Continued

1. In a large bowl, combine butter, sugars and peanut butter.
2. Add eggs and vanilla and mix well.
3. Add flour, baking soda and salt and mix well.
4. Roll dough into balls the size of a golf ball. Place balls about 2" (5 cm) apart on an ungreased cookie sheet. Press down balls with a fork dipped in flour.
5. Bake at 350°F (180°C) for 10 minutes, or until golden brown. Remove cookies to a cooling rack.

Makes 3-4 dozen cookies.

NOTE: Chopped peanuts may be added for extra crunch.

Barb's Chocolate Toffee Squares

The chocolate bar — reinvented!

1 cup	butter OR margarine	250 mL
1 cup	brown sugar	250 mL
1	egg yolk	1
2 tsp.	vanilla	10 mL
1¾ cups+2 tbsp.	flour	455 mL
6 x 1½ oz.	Jersey Milk chocolate bars	6 x 45 g
½ cup	sliced OR slivered almonds	125 mL

1. Cream together butter and sugar.
2. Add egg yolk and vanilla and mix well.
3. Gradually beat in flour and knead well.
4. Spread batter in a 10 x 15" (25 x 38 cm) jelly roll pan.
5. Bake at 350°F (180°C) for 15 minutes. The pastry should be light brown and puffy.
6. Place 6 Jersey Milk chocolate bars on the hot pastry; let chocolate melt for 5 minutes, then spread.
7. Sprinkle sliced or slivered almonds on top.

Makes 30 squares.

Crispy Crunch Bars

The name says it all. This tastes like a Crispy Crunch chocolate bar.

Base:

½ cup	butter OR margarine	125 mL
½ cup	white sugar	125 mL
½ cup	brown sugar	125 mL
1	egg	1
½ cup	smooth peanut butter	125 mL
1 cup	flour	250 mL
¼ tsp.	baking powder	1 mL
½ tsp.	salt	2 mL
½ tsp.	vanilla	2 mL
1 cup	rolled oats	250 mL
1 cup	chocolate chips	250 mL

Peanut Butter Icing:

½ cup	icing sugar	125 mL
¼ cup	milk	60 mL
¼ cup	smooth peanut butter	60 mL

1. Cream together butter and sugars. Add egg and peanut butter and mix until well blended.
2. Combine flour, baking powder and salt. Add to creamed mixture.
3. Stir in vanilla and oats.
4. Spread batter in a greased 9 x 13" (23 x 33 cm) pan.
5. Bake at 350°F (180°C) for 25 minutes. Remove from oven.
6. Immediately sprinkle chocolate chips on the hot cake
7. While chips are melting on the cake, combine the icing ingredients. Pour icing over cake and swirl melted chocolate with icing to give a marbled appearance.

Makes 24 bars.

God of goodness, bless our food.
Keep us in a pleasant mood.
Bless the cook and all who serve us.
From indigestion, Lord, preserve us.

Sour Cream Raisin Bars

This surprising little bar is a wallflower. It doesn't have as much eye appeal as some, but it tastes absolutely wonderful.

Base:

1 cup	butter OR margarine	250 mL
1 cup	brown sugar	250 mL
1¾ cups	flour	425 mL
1 tsp.	baking soda	5 mL
1¾ cups	rolled oats	425 mL

Raisin Filling:

1½ cups	brown sugar	375 mL
3 tbsp.	cornstarch	45 mL
4	egg yolks, beaten	4
2 cups	sour cream	500 mL
2 cups	raisins	500 mL
1 tsp.	vanilla	5 mL

1. To prepare the base, cream together butter and sugar. Add flour and baking soda and mix well. Add rolled oats.
2. Set aside ½ cup (125 mL) of crumb mixture for topping.
3. Pat the remainder into a greased 9 x 13" (23 x 33 cm) pan. Bake at 350°F (180°C) for 15 minutes.
4. To make the filling, mix sugar and cornstarch with egg yolks. Add sour cream and raisins.
5. Bring to a boil over medium heat, stirring constantly. Simmer over low heat until mixture thickens, about 5 minutes. Watch it very carefully, as it scorches easily.
6. Remove the raisin mixture from the heat and stir in the vanilla.
7. Pour onto the baked crust. Top with reserved crumbs.
8. Bake at 350°F (180°C) for 20 minutes.

Makes 24 bars.

Butter Tart Squares

I love butter tarts, but I rarely find time to make them. These are easy, and just as gooey delicious! This smaller amount is how the recipe came to me, but I always double it!

Base:

½ cup	butter OR margarine	125 mL
2 tbsp.	icing sugar	30 mL
1½ cups	flour	375 mL

Filling:

1½ cups	brown sugar	375 mL
¼ cup	melted butter OR margarine	60 mL
2	eggs, beaten	2
1 tbsp.	vinegar	15 mL
1 tsp.	vanilla	5 mL
1 cup	raisins	250 mL

1. To prepare the base, cream together butter and sugar. Blend in flour. It will be crumbly.
2. Turn crumbs into an ungreased 9" (23 cm) square pan and pat down.
3. Bake in a 350°F (180°C) oven for 5 minutes.
4. To make the filling, mix all the ingredients together and beat with an electric mixer or wire whisk. Pour over the base.
5. Bake at 350°F (180°C) for 30 minutes. Bake just until filling is set (just until it doesn't jiggle in the center).

Makes 16 squares.

NOTE: DOUBLE the whole recipe for a 9 x 13" (23 x 33 cm) pan and increase baking time by 10 minutes.

See photograph on the back cover.

An angler was hauled into court, charged with catching 18 more bass than the law permitted.

"Guilty or not guilty?" demanded the judge.

"Guilty, Your Honor," declared the young man.

"Ten dollars and costs," pronounced the judge.

The defendant paid the fine, then asked cheerfully, "And now, Your Honor, may I have several typewritten copies of the court record to take back home and show to my friends?"

Date Squares

I've never quite understood why this is often called matrimonial cake. Perhaps because several "dates" lead to marriage. Whatever you call it, this is a date-lover's delight!

Date Filling:

2 cups	chopped dates	500 mL
2 cups	water	500 mL
1 tsp.	cinnamon	5 mL
1 tsp.	lemon juice	5 mL

Base and Topping:

1 cup	butter OR margarine	250 mL
1 cup	brown sugar	250 mL
2 cups	flour	500 mL
½ tsp.	salt	2 mL
1 tsp.	baking soda	5 mL
2 cups	rolled oats	500 mL

1. Put all filling ingredients in a saucepan, bring to a boil and simmer, stirring occasionally, until dates are completely soft. Add more water as necessary to prevent burning.
2. To make crust and topping, cream together butter and sugar.
3. Mix flour, salt and baking soda. Add to creamed mixture.
4. Add oats and mix well.
5. Spread a little more than half of the base mixture in a greased, 9 x 13" (23 x 33 cm) pan. Pat down firmly.
6. Spread date filling over the base.
7. Sprinkle the remaining crumb mixture evenly over the filling. Press down slightly.
8. Bake in a 350°F (180°C) oven for ½ hour, or until lightly browned.
9. Cool in the pan. Cut and serve.

Makes 24 squares.

For every cup and plateful
God make us truly grateful.
A.S.T. Fisher

Jam Snacks

(MARIE) When I first started talking about a cookbook, a friend of my son's said, "I sure hope Jam Snacks are going to be in it." He used to trade Drew for them at lunchtime at school. So, these are for you, Vance!

Base:

1 cup	flour	250 mL
1 tsp.	baking powder	5 mL
½ cup	butter OR margarine	125 mL
3 tbsp.	milk	45 mL
1	egg, beaten	1
⅔ cup	raspberry jam*	150 mL

Topping:

1¼ cups	unsweetened, desiccated coconut	300 mL
¾ cup	sugar	175 mL
1	egg, beaten	1
½ tsp.	vanilla	2 mL
1½ tbsp.	butter OR margarine, melted	22 mL

1. The base ingredients must be mixed by hand, but it is easy. To make the base, combine flour, baking powder and butter with a pastry blender until finely blended.
2. Mix the milk with the beaten egg, and add to the flour mixture, mixing it in with a fork. This batter will be very thick and sticky.
3. Spread batter in a well-greased and floured 8" (20 cm) square pan.
4. Spread a layer of raspberry jam over this layer.
5. Mix all topping ingredients together. Carefully drop by spoonfuls over the jam until the jam is well covered.
6. Bake at 325°F (160C°) for 40 minutes, or until topping is golden brown. Let cool. Cut into squares. Delicious!

Makes 16 Jam Snacks.

NOTE: For a 9 x 13" (23 x 33 cm) pan, double all ingredients and increase baking time by 10 minutes.

* Substitute any jam you have on hand (but a jelly won't work!).

See photograph on the back cover.

  *Stop and Snack Awhile*

Saucepan Brownies — No Icing

You will make these brownies entirely in the saucepan. So, this is for those of you who are "dishwashing-resistant", or simply in a hurry. The results will be impossible to resist.

½ cup	butter OR margarine	125 mL
2 x 1 oz.	squares unsweetened chocolate	2 x 30 g
1 cup	sugar	250 mL
½ cup	flour	125 mL
1 tsp.	baking powder	5 mL
1 tsp.	vanilla	5 mL
½ cup	chopped walnuts	125 mL
2	eggs	2
	icing sugar	

1. Melt together butter and chocolate in a saucepan over low heat, stirring constantly. Remove from heat.
2. Stir in sugar, flour, baking powder, vanilla and walnuts.
3. Add eggs and beat thoroughly.
4. Spread in greased 9" (23 cm) square pan.
5. Bake in 350°F (180°C) oven for 30 minutes or until done. Cool in pan on a cooling rack.
6. When cool, dust with icing sugar and cut into squares.

Makes 16 brownies.

SERVING SUGGESTIONS: These are good eaten right from the pan or topped with ice cream and chocolate sauce for dessert!

Attention Raisin Lovers!

Helen's husband, Doug, likes these with raisins instead of nuts. So sometimes we humor him. We wouldn't want to tell him so, but they're still mighty good!

Chocolate Cream Cheese Brownies

A little more complicated brownie for those special occasions when you really want to show people that they're special too. A favorite in the Webber family.

Chocolate Layer:

1 cup	chocolate chips	250 mL
3 tbsp.	butter OR margarine	45 mL
2	eggs	2
¾ cup	white sugar	175 mL
½ cup	flour	125 mL
½ tsp.	baking powder	2 mL
½ tsp.	salt	2 mL
½ cup	chopped walnuts	125 mL
1 tsp.	vanilla	5 mL
¼ tsp.	almond extract	1 mL

Cream Cheese Layer:

2 tbsp.	butter OR margarine, softened	30 mL
4 oz.	pkg. cream cheese, softened	125 g
¼ cup	white sugar	60 mL
1	egg	1
1 tbsp.	flour	15 mL
1 tsp.	vanilla	5 mL

1. TO MAKE THE CHOCOLATE LAYER, melt chocolate chips and butter in the top of a double boiler or over low heat in a nonstick pan, stirring constantly. To microwave, be sure the heat is very low; watch it carefully. It must melt smoothly and it mustn't boil. Set aside to cool.
2. In another bowl, beat eggs and sugar until well-blended.
3. Sift flour, baking powder and salt into egg mixture. Beat well.
4. Stir melted chocolate, which has been allowed to cool, walnuts, vanilla and almond extract into egg mixture.
5. TO MAKE THE CREAM CHEESE LAYER, in a medium-sized bowl, cream together butter and cream cheese until fluffy.
6. Blend sugar, egg, flour and vanilla into the creamed mixture. Set aside.
7. TO PUT IT ALL TOGETHER, spread HALF of the chocolate mixture evenly in the bottom of a greased 9" (23 cm) square pan.
8. Spread the cream cheese mixture over the chocolate layer.
9. Drop spoonfuls of remaining chocolate over the cream cheese. Swirl with a fork for a marbled effect.
10. Bake at 350°F (180°C) for 40-50 minutes, or until a toothpick inserted near the center comes out clean.

Makes 24 brownies.

NOTE: Double all ingredients for a 9 x 13" (23 x 33 cm) pan. We do!

Stop and Snack Awhile

Turtle Brownies

The Ninja Turtles would give up pizza for these!

19 oz.	German chocolate cake mix	520 g
3/4 cup	melted butter OR margarine	175 mL
1/3 cup	evaporated milk	75 mL
2 cups	caramels (1 large package)	500 mL
1/3 cup	evaporated milk	75 mL
1 cup	chopped pecans OR walnuts	250 mL
1/2 cup	chocolate chips OR more	125 ml.

1. Mix the chocolate cake mix with melted butter and evaporated milk.
2. Spread HALF the batter mixture in a 9 x 13" (23 x 33 cm) pan. Bake in a 350°F (180°C) oven for 8-10 minutes.
3. Over low heat, melt the caramels with 1/3 cup (75 mL) of the milk, stirring constantly to prevent scorching. OR microwave on high 3-4 minutes, stirring once.
4. Layer the nuts, chocolate chips and caramel mixture over the chocolate base.
5. By spoonfuls, drop the remaining chocolate batter over the contents of the pan, to cover as evenly as possible. The batter will spread when baked.
6. Bake in a 350°F (180°C) oven 15-18 minutes.

Makes 3 dozen brownies.

SERVING SUGGESTIONS: Cut into squares, while still warm! Let cool before serving. Store, covered, at room temperature.

See photograph on the back cover.

Thanks for breakfast, lunch and dinner,
If it weren't for you, I'd be much thinner.
J. Stubbs

Mocha-Iced Brownies

A traditional brownie with a nice twist for coffee lovers.

1 cup	butter OR margarine	250 mL
1 cup	white sugar	250 mL
2	eggs	2
¼ cup	cocoa powder	60 mL
2 tsp.	vanilla	10 mL
1 cup	flour	250 mL
¼ tsp.	salt	1 mL
1 cup	chopped nuts	250 mL

1. Cream together the butter, sugar and eggs. Add the cocoa, blending thoroughly. Add the vanilla.
2. Add the flour and salt to the creamed mixture, beating well. Add the chopped nuts.
3. Spread the batter in a greased 7 x 11" (18 x 28 cm) cake pan, or one of approximately the same size.
4. Bake at 300°F (150°C) for 30 minutes. Do not overbake. Center should be barely set.
5. Prepare Mocha Icing, below, and spread on cooled cake.

Makes 18 iced brownies.

Mocha Icing

1½ cups	icing sugar	375 mL
3 tbsp.	cocoa powder	45 mL
3 tbsp.	butter OR margarine, softened	45 mL
3 tbsp.	strong, hot coffee	45 mL

1. Sift together icing sugar and cocoa, add butter and coffee and mix well to make a thin icing.

Makes about 1 cup (250 mL) of icing.

SERVING SUGGESTION: Allow the icing to set before serving these. They are good the first day but better the second day.

 *Stop and Snack Awhile*

Marie's Ski Cake

(MARIE) We have no idea where this name came from, but we've called it that for too long to change it. This is my son Todd's favorite. Now, there's a young man with very good taste!

Cake Layer:

½ cup	butter OR margarine	125 mL
½ cup	white sugar	125 mL
2 cups	flour	500 mL
1 tbsp.	baking powder	15 ml.
1 tsp.	vanilla	5 ml
1 cup	milk	250 mL
⅔ cup	chocolate chips	150 mL
2	egg whites	2
½ cup	white sugar	125 mL

Icing Layer:

½ cup	butter OR margarine, room temperature	125 mL
1½ cups	icing sugar, sifted	375 mL
2	egg yolks	2

Chocolate Layer:

1 cup	chocolate chips	250 mL

1. To make the cake layer, cream together butter and sugar in a large mixing bowl.
2. In a separate bowl, mix flour with baking powder.
3. In a measuring cup, add vanilla to milk
4. Add flour and milk mixtures alternately to creamed mixture, beating well after each addition. Batter will be thick and sticky.
5. Pour chocolate chips over batter, but don't mix yet.
6. In a separate bowl, beat egg whites until stiff. Add ½ cup (125 mL) sugar and beat until well blended.
7. BY HAND, fold egg whites and chocolate chips into the batter. The resulting mixture will be lumpy. Don't overmix!
8. Spread the batter in a greased 9 x 13" (23 x 33 cm) pan.
9. Bake at 350°F (180°C) for 30 minutes. Remove the cake from the oven and let it cool completely.
10. Combine icing ingredients and spread on cooled cake.
11. Melt chocolate chips over low heat, stirring constantly to prevent scorching. OR microwave for 4 minutes over medium heat, stirring once. Pour over icing and spread carefully. Cover and refrigerate until ready to serve.

Serves 24.

See photograph on the back cover.

Zucchini Chocolate Cake

A really good snackin' cake —and no calories (in the zucchini)!

2¼ cups	flour	550 mL
¼ cup	cocoa	60 mL
1 tsp.	baking soda	5 mL
1 tsp.	salt	5 mL
½ cup	butter OR margarine, softened	125 mL
½ cup	vegetable oil	125 mL
1¾ cups	white sugar	425 mL
2	eggs	2
1 tsp.	vanilla	5 mL
½ cup	buttermilk*	125 mL
2 cups	grated, unpared zucchini	500 mL
6 oz.	pkg. chocolate chips	170 g
¾ cup	chopped walnuts	175 mL

1. In a small bowl, combine the flour, cocoa, baking soda and salt.
2. In a large mixing bowl, cream together the butter, oil, sugar, eggs and vanilla.
3. Add the dry ingredients to the creamed mixture, alternately with the buttermilk.
4. Stir in zucchini.
5. Pour batter into a greased 9 x 13" (23 x 33 cm) pan.
6. Sprinkle chocolate chips and walnuts evenly over the batter.
7. Bake in a 325°F oven (160°C) for 55 minutes. Do not overbake.

Serves 15.

* *You may substitute ½ cup (125 mL) milk mixed with 2 tsp. (10 mL) lemon juice or vinegar.*

"Gus," said Bill, as he caught up with Gus on the way back to camp, "are all the rest of the boys out of the woods yet?"

"Yes," said Gus.

"All six of them?"

"Yes, all six of them."

"And they're all safe?"

"Yep," answered Gus, "they're all safe."

"Then," said Bill, his chest swelling, "I've shot a deer."

Stop and Snack Awhile

Tomato Soup Cake

Don't let the tomato soup fool you. This is a delicious, moist spice cake with an attractive orange color.

¼ cup	butter OR margarine, softened	60 mL
1 cup	white sugar	250 mL
1	egg	1
10 oz.	can tomato soup	284 mL
1½ cups	flour	375 mL
2 tsp.	baking soda	10 mL
½ tsp.	cinnamon	2 mL
½ tsp.	cloves	2 mL
½ tsp.	nutmeg	2 mL
½ tsp.	allspice	2 mL
¼ tsp.	salt	1 mL
1 cup	raisins	250 mL

1. Cream together butter and sugar. Add egg and tomato soup and mix well. The batter will be a little lumpy.
2. Mix all the dry ingredients together until well blended. Add to the creamed mixture. Mix well.
3. Stir in raisins.
4. Spread the batter in a greased 8" (20 cm) square pan.
5. Bake at 350°F (180°) for 50-60 minutes, or until a toothpick inserted in the center of the cake comes out dry.

Serves 9.

SERVING SUGGESTION: Let cake cool and ice with Butter Icing, below.

VARIATION: For a 9 x 13" (23 x 33 cm) cake, double all the ingredients, except raisins, which you increase to 1½ cups (375 mL).

Butter Icing

1½ cups	icing sugar	375 mL
3 tbsp.	butter OR margarine	45 mL
4 tsp.	milk	20 mL
1 tsp.	vanilla	5 mL

1. Mix all ingredients together. Add more milk if needed. Spread over cooled cake.

Makes about 1 cup (250 mL) of icing.

Rhubarb Cake

Some of our American guests don't know what rhubarb is. All we can say is that it is a very, very tart plant, of which we eat the stalk — and which makes fantastic pies and cakes. In some areas it is known as pieplant because it makes such wonderful pies. We often combine rhubarb with strawberries and in Britain ginger and apples are often added to complement the rhubarb flavor. This version makes a good snackin' cake.

½ cup	butter OR margarine	125 mL
1½ cups	white sugar	375 mL
1	egg	1
1 tsp.	vanilla	5 mL
2 cups	flour	500 mL
1 tsp.	baking soda	5 mL
1 cup	buttermilk*	250 mL
2 cups	chopped rhubarb	500 mL

Topping:

¼ cup	butter OR margarine	60 mL
2 tsp.	cinnamon	10 mL
1 cup	brown sugar	250 mL

1. Cream together butter and sugar. Add egg and vanilla and beat well.
2. Mix flour and baking soda. Add to creamed mixture alternately with buttermilk.
3. Fold in rhubarb.
4. Spread batter in a greased, 9 x 13" (23 x 33 cm) pan.
5. Mix topping ingredients until crumbly. Sprinkle evenly over batter.
6. Bake at 350°F (180°C) for 30 minutes. Let the cake cool in the pan.

Serves 15.

* *For buttermilk, substitute 1 tbsp. (15 mL) lemon juice or vinegar in milk, to make up 1 cup (250 mL) OR substitute ½ cup (125 mL) sour cream and ½ cup (125 mL) milk.*

 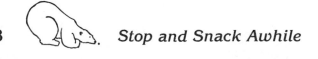

Taste Teasers

Every day is a special occasion at North Knife Lake. When the guests arrive from their day of fishing they are treated to a cocktail hour along with a selection of our favorite appetizers. We've come a long way from the days of the rustic fishing camp!

Chili Cheese Log

This is so easy, you'll never believe how good it tastes! These will keep in the refrigerator for 2-3 weeks, we're told. We've never had a chance to find out!

3 cups	grated Cheddar cheese	750 mL
4 oz.	cream cheese, softened	125 g
1 tsp.	Worcestershire sauce	5 mL
½ tsp.	garlic powder	2 mL
¼ tsp.	salt	1 mL
	chili powder — Lots!	

1. Combine the first 5 ingredients. Divide the mixture in half and roll each half into a log with a diameter about 1½" (4 cm).
2. Sprinkle a piece of waxed paper liberally with chili powder. Roll the cheese logs in the chili powder, one at a time, until they are completely coated with chili powder.
3. Wrap the logs in waxed paper and store them in a plastic bag.
4. Chill in refrigerator 3-4 days or overnight to blend flavors.

Makes 2 logs about 8" (20 cm) long.

Smoked Trout Pâté

OK, so you don't keep smoked trout in your pantry. This is a versatile recipe and will work with any kind of smoked fish or with canned salmon and liquid smoke. It's OK to cheat! Especially when the result is great flavor.

4 oz.	cream cheese, softened	125 g
2 tsp.	grated onion	10 mL
1 tsp.	lemon juice	5 mL
½-1 tsp.	horseradish, more or less to taste	2-5 mL
⅛ tsp.	salt	0.5 mL
1 cup	flaked smoked trout OR other smoked fish OR 7½ oz. (225 g) salmon, drained and ½ tsp. (2 mL) liquid smoke	250 mL

1. Mash cream cheese with onion and lemon juice. Add the lesser amount of horseradish, plus salt and fish. Taste; add horseradish, if desired.
2. Chill a few hours before using.

Makes about 1½ cups (375 mL).

SERVING SUGGESTION: Serve with assorted crackers or thinly sliced dark rye or pumpernickel bread.

See photograph on page 103.

Taste Teasers

Our Own Spinach Dip

Sometimes when we find a recipe that we want to make, we don't have all the ingredients it calls for. Since both the lodges are isolated, the missing ingredients aren't that easy to come by and we are forced to experiment. This might be a familiar recipe, but we think our simplified version is just as good as the original.

10 oz.	pkg. frozen spinach	283 g
1 cup	mayonnaise	250 mL
1 cup	sour cream	250 mL
¼ cup	chopped green onion	60 mL
1 tsp.	salt	5 mL
½ tsp.	DLS* OR your favorite steak seasoning	2 mL
2 tbsp.	dried (OR chopped fresh) parsley	30 mL
5 oz.	can water chestnuts, chopped	150 g

1. Thaw spinach thoroughly. Drain it through a strainer, squeezing out as much juice as possible. Chop it into bite-sized pieces.
2. Mix spinach with all the other ingredients and chill.

Makes about 3 cups (750 mL) of dip.

SERVING SUGGESTION: We often serve it chilled, in a bowl, surrounded by pieces of French bread. But, if you are able to purchase or bake a round loaf of bread, this is very nice served warm in the hollowed-out loaf. To serve warm, hollow out a loaf of bread, keeping the top slice in one piece for a lid. Spoon dip into the loaf, cover with the lid and wrap with aluminum foil. Bake at 300°F (150°C) for 2 hours. Serve hot with the pieces of bread for dipping. You may also heat the dip in a covered casserole and serve it warm with assorted crackers and raw vegetables.

* *Dymond Lake Seasoning*

Fisherman's Surprise Spread

This is one of our most requested recipes, and IF the guests leave any, the staff finishes it off very quickly. Make it a day ahead or the same day.

8 oz.	cream cheese, softened	250 g
½ cup	sour cream	125 mL
¼ cup	mayonnaise	60 mL
2 x 4 oz.	cans broken shrimp, rinsed and drained	2 x 113 g
8 oz.	jar seafood cocktail sauce	227 g
2 cups	shredded mozzarella cheese	500 mL
1	green pepper, chopped	1
3	green onions, chopped	3
1	tomato, chopped	1

1. Mix the first 3 ingredients together. Spread over a 12" (30 cm) pizza pan, or a similar-sized dish.
2. Add a layer of each the rest of the ingredients, in the order given.
3. Cover and chill until ready to serve. Serve with crackers, Melba toast or Toast Cups, below.

Serves 30.

SERVING SUGGESTION: If you have any spread left over, mix it up and spread it on a bun or French bread. Eat it warm or cold!

VARIATION: Crab may be substituted for shrimp and chunky salsa may be substituted for the seafood cocktail spread.

Toast Cups

Cut crusts from slices of white bread (sandwich bread is the best shape). Cut each slice into 4 squares. Press each square into SMALL, ungreased muffin cups. Bake at 350°F (180°C), on the bottom rack, for about 15 minutes, until the corners are well browned. Remove, cool and store in a plastic bag. They keep indefinitely. These are a delicious and easy substitute for tart or puff shells for many appetizer fillings.

Taste Teasers — Wild and Tame

Gavin's Caribou Strips, page 9
Fruit Sauce, page 8
Pizza Roll-Ups, page 108
Wild Meatball Taste Teasers, page 8
Fish Balls, page 25

Goose Tidbits, page 16
Duck Taste Teaser with Bacon
*   and Water Chestnuts, page 19*
Shrimp Puffs, page 107
Smoked Trout Pâté, page 100

Mexican Bean Dip

One night we were scrambling for a Taste Teaser at North Knife Lake, and after taking stock of what leftovers and supplies we had, this is what we came up with. We like the flavor of the bacon in this one and we think you'll like it too.

14 oz.	can hot and spicy refried beans	398 mL
8 oz.	pkg. cream cheese	250 g
1 cup	sour cream	250 mL
1	garlic clove, crushed, OR ¼ tsp. (1 mL) garlic powder	1
1 lb.	bacon, cooked crisp and crumbled	500 g
½ cup	chopped green onion	125 mL
1 cup	chopped tomato	250 mL
1 cup	salsa (mild, OR hot — your choice!)	250 mL
	grated Cheddar cheese — enough to cover top	

1. In a 9 x 13" (23 x 33 cm) casserole (or a flat round dish, or a pizza pan) layer the ingredients in the following order:
   - refried beans
   - cream cheese mixed with sour cream and garlic
   - crumbled bacon
   - chopped green onion
   - chopped tomato
   - salsa
   - grated Cheddar

Serves 12-20 people.

SERVING SUGGESTION: Serve hot or cold. This is a layered dip that goes well with nacho chips. For you hot 'n' spicy fans, add a little Tabasco sauce or cayenne pepper to the refried beans. Most of us like it just as it is.

A Fisherman's Lament

A three-pound pull, and a five-pound bite;
An eight-pound jump, and a ten-pound fight;
A twelve-pound bend to your pole, but alas!
When you get him aboard, he's a half-pound bass!

Berry Pickers –

Marie and Helen return from some successful berry picking with their trusty "bear alert" dogs, Daisy and Sheba.

Nachos Suprême

For an easy hors d'oeuvre, bring out the bag of nachos, arrange them on a platter and get creative.

nacho chips
chopped tomatoes
salsa
chopped green OR ripe olives
finely chopped jalapeño peppers
chopped green onion
crumbled bacon
grated Cheddar OR mozzarella cheese

1. Arrange nacho chips on a large ovenproof platter or plate.
2. On top of the nacho chips, scatter as many of the toppings as you wish. Top with grated Cheddar and/or mozzarella cheese.
3. Pop the platter in the microwave or in the oven at 350°F (180°C) until the cheese melts.

SERVING SUGGESTION: Serve with sour cream and salsa for dipping.

Polynesian Mushrooms

Fresh mushrooms are always available making this a year round taste teaser.

24	fresh medium mushrooms	24
¼ cup	butter OR margarine	60 mL
1	garlic clove, crushed	1
¼ cup	shredded mozzarella cheese	60 mL
	mushroom stems, finely chopped	
2 tbsp.	milk	30 mL
1 tsp.	soy sauce	5 mL
½ cup	dry bread crumbs	125 mL

1. Gently remove stems from mushrooms. Set mushroom caps aside.
2. In a small saucepan, over medium heat, combine all remaining ingredients. Stir well to melt butter.
3. Fill mushroom caps and arrange them on a baking sheet.
4. Broil for 3-4 minutes OR bake at 350°F (180°C) for 5-10 minutes, until heated through and cheese is melted. Serve hot.

Serves 12.

Taste Teasers

Shrimp Puffs

This makes 2-3 dozen puffs, which can be warmed and eaten immediately or frozen for future use.

Puffs:

1 cup	water	250 mL
½ cup	butter OR margarine	125 mL
1 cup	flour	250 mL
½ tsp.	salt	2 mL
4	eggs	4

Shrimp Filling:

8 oz.	cream cheese	250 g
⅓ cup	mayonnaise	75 mL
½ tsp.	garlic salt	2 mL
½ cup	finely chopped onion	125 mL
7.5 oz.	can broken shrimp	113 g

1. Preheat oven to 375°F (190°C).
2. In a medium-sized saucepan, bring water and butter to a boil.
3. Add the flour and salt all at once, and, stirring vigorously, cook over medium heat until the mixture sticks together and forms a ball. (This happens very quickly.)
4. Remove the saucepan from the heat. Let the mixture cool for 2 minutes.
5. Add the unbeaten eggs 1 at a time, beating each time with a wooden spoon until the egg is completely absorbed into the batter. When finished, the batter will be smooth and glossy.
6. Drop batter by rounded teaspoonfuls (10 mL) onto a greased cookie sheet.
7. Bake at 375°F (190°C) for 15 minutes, or until slightly browned. (Too long a time is better than too short a time.)
8. Let puffs cool while you mix all the filling ingredients together well.
9. Cut slits on the sides of the cooled puffs, near the top, creating a lid that can be opened.
10. Stuff the puffs with the filling.
11. Cover and refrigerate or freeze until ready to use.
12. If they are not frozen, heat them at 350°F (180°C) for 10 minutes. If you have frozen them, do not thaw but extend the heating time to 15-20 minutes.

Makes 2-3 dozen puffs.

See photograph on page 103.

Pizza Roll-Ups

The best time to make these is when you are making buns or bread. Just use some of your dough, after it has risen once. We'll assume that you don't start your day by putting dough to rise. In that case, follow the following recipe!

Dough:

1½ cups	lukewarm water	375 mL
2 tbsp.	oil	30 mL
1 tsp.	salt	5 mL
1 tbsp.	instant yeast	15 mL
3-4 cups	flour (approximately)	750 mL-1 L

Pizza Filling:

1 cup	ketchup	250 mL
1	medium onion, finely chopped	1
1	small green pepper, finely chopped	1
10 oz.	can mushrooms, drained and chopped	284 mL
4-8 oz.	pepperoni, finely chopped	115-250 g
1 cup	grated Cheddar cheese	250 mL
1 tsp.	dried oregano	5 mL
1 tsp.	dried basil	5 mL
1 tsp.	DLS* OR your favorite steak seasoning	5 mL

1. To make the dough, put water and oil in a mixing bowl.
2. In a separate bowl, mix yeast and salt with 3 cups (750 mL) of flour.
3. Add the flour mixture to the liquids. Then, by hand (or machine, if you have one) work in enough remaining flour to make a smooth, not sticky mixture. Place the dough in a greased bowl to rise.
4. Combine the pizza filling ingredients.
5. To put it all together, divide the dough in half. Roll out half the dough into an 8 x 18" (20 x 45 cm) rectangle.
6. Spread half the pizza filling on the dough.
7. Starting at the long side, roll up the dough. You now have a roll that is 18" (45 cm) long. Cut the roll in ⅜" (1 cm) slices.
8. Place each slice, flat side down, on a greased baking sheet.
9. Bake at 400°F (200°C) for 15 minutes, or until lightly browned. Do not overbake. The bottoms tend to get brown very quickly, so if you have 2 pans in the oven at once, switch the pans halfway through.
10. These freeze very nicely. Reheat frozen roll-ups for 5-10 minutes before serving. Watch them closely, because they burn easily.

This will make 7-8 dozen Roll-Ups.

* *Dymond Lake Seasoning*

See photograph on page 103.

Taste Teasers

Chicken Strips with Honey Dill Sauce

Give yourself a little time to prepare this, as the batter should be made ahead. The sauce can also be prepared early, but the deep frying is done at the last minute, just before serving.

Batter:

2	eggs	2
1 tbsp.	cooking oil	15 mL
1⅓ cups	flour	325 mL
1 tsp.	baking powder	5 mL
1 tsp.	salt	5 mL
½ tsp.	DLS* OR ¼ tsp. (1 mL) pepper	2 mL
¾ cup	water	175 mL
3	chicken breasts, boneless and thawed	3
	flour	
	fat for deep-frying	

1. To make the batter, beat the eggs until frothy.
2. Stir in the rest of the batter ingredients.
3. Store the batter in a covered container in the refrigerator for 2-10 hours.
4. Cut chicken in finger-sized strips. Dredge with flour.
5. Dip chicken in chilled batter and deep-fry in 375°F (190°C) fat until golden brown on both sides. This only takes about 2 minutes.

Serves 12.

SERVING SUGGESTION: Serve with Honey Dill Sauce, below.

* Dymond Lake Seasoning

Honey Dill Sauce

1½ cups	mayonnaise	375 mL
1 cup	liquid honey	250 mL
2 tsp.	dried dillweed	10 mL

1. Combine all ingredients and serve with chicken strips.

Makes 2½ cups (625 mL) of sauce.

SERVING SUGGESTION: A delicious dip with anything you deep-fry!

Jeanne's Magic Disappearing Chicken Wings

(and Helen's and Marie's and all their kids'!)
This is just an all-round favorite!

3 lbs.	chicken wings	1.5 kg
1 cup	flour	250 mL
1 tsp.	DLS* OR ½ tsp. (2 mL) salt and ½ tsp. (2 mL) pepper	5 mL
3	eggs, beaten	3

Tangy Sauce:

3 tbsp.	soy sauce	45 mL
3 tbsp.	water	45 mL
¾ cup	white sugar	175 mL
½ cup	vinegar	125 mL
½ tsp.	salt	2 mL

1. Cut off wing tips and discard or freeze for another use. Cut remaining wings in 2 pieces. (You will now have 1 piece that looks like a tiny drumstick, and 1 piece that still looks like a wing — sort of.)
2. Mix flour with DLS* in a small, shallow pan.
3. Dip wings in beaten egg, then roll in flour mixture.
4. Place wings on a well-oiled baking sheet and bake at 400°F (200°C) for ½ hour, or until well browned.
5. Remove the wings to a casserole or roaster.
6. Combine all sauce ingredients and pour evenly over wings.
7. Bake, UNCOVERED, at 350°F (180°C) for 1 hour. Stir once during baking.

Serves 18-20 as a taste teaser or 8 for dinner.

SERVING SUGGESTION: At home, we serve these as a meal with rice. This also makes a great dish to take to a potluck supper.

NOTE: These are best when the sauce thickens and becomes sticky. Make lots! These wings do a disappearing act!

* *Dymond Lake Seasoning*

Mushroom Turnovers

(MARIE) The first time I tasted Mushroom Turnovers, Helen and Doug were visiting, and Helen made a surprise dinner for us. The four of us demolished this complete recipe. The guests at the Lodge are a fraction more polite!

Cream Cheese Pastry:

8 oz.	cream cheese, softened	250 g
½ cup	butter OR margarine, softened	125 mL
1½ cups	flour	375 mL

Mushroom Filling:

3 tbsp.	butter OR margarine	45 mL
1	large onion, chopped	1
2 x 10 oz.	cans mushrooms, drained and chopped	2 x 284 g
2 tbsp.	flour	30 mL
1 tsp.	salt	5 mL
¼ tsp.	pepper	1 mL
¼ tsp.	dried thyme	1 mL
¼ cup	sour cream	60 mL
1	egg, beaten	1

1. Mix butter and cheese together well. Add flour and shape dough into a ball. Chill at least 1 hour.
2. While you're waiting, prepare the filling. Combine butter, onion and mushrooms in a frying pan. Sauté for about 10 minutes, until tender.
3. Add the rest of the ingredients, except the egg. Stir until thickened, then remove from heat. Cool completely.
4. To make the turnovers, roll out the pastry fairly thin onto a lightly floured surface.
5. Cut pastry into 3" (7 cm) rounds.
6. Place 1 tsp. (5 mL) of filling in the center of each circle.
7. Brush half of the outer edge of the pastry circle with beaten egg.
8. Fold circle over and press edges together with a fork or fingers to seal.
9. Arrange turnovers on a greased baking sheet. Cut tiny slits in the top of each.
10. Brush tops with beaten egg.
11. Bake at 450°F (230°C) for about 10 minutes, or until golden brown. Serve hot.

Makes 3-4 dozen turnovers.

NOTE: These freeze well, either before or after they are baked. Bake frozen, for 10-15 minutes. To freeze before baking, lay turnovers on a waxed paper-lined tray. Freeze, then remove from paper and store in a zip-lock bag in freezer.

Grin and Bare It

(HELEN) We had a group of naturalists at Dymond Lake one very hot July day. Bonnie, our resident naturalist was taking the group up to North River, a five-mile boat ride. They would be gone at least twelve hours though as they would have to wait for high tide on Hudson Bay to come back. Bob, one of the group, had a bad back and didn't think he should make the trip. Callie, his wife, felt sorry for him and volunteered to stay behind with him. Thus began their thrill of a lifetime!

They spent the morning out photographing the abundance of wild flowers that were blooming, checking out the berries and adding to their bird checklists. But after lunch, Bob was feeling badly at the thought of what they were missing. He figured the others would come back with all kinds of stories about the neat things they had seen and done. But, being a good sport, he agreed to go out for a walk with Callie.

Around two o'clock they came back to the cabin to take a shower. Now that was back in the days when the shower was nothing more than a chipboard lean-to tacked on the side of the cabin. One good burst of wind and it could have gone flying. Bob put on his pajamas to walk through the cabin and headed outside to the shower. About five minutes later, Callie headed out to climb in while the water was still running.

The next thing I heard was Bob yelling, "polar bear!" Well, I really didn't pay too much attention. After all, it was July and not exactly bear season. I thought Bob was just trying to get Callie to come streaking through the cabin, naked. But all of a sudden they were both yelling, "Helen, there is a bear out here!" Well, that got my attention!

I yelled at them to stay put until I could see what the bear had in mind. I opened the door of the cabin and here was not one but THREE bears! — a mother and her two, year-old cubs and they weren't twenty feet from me! As I stood gaping, that big momma swung her head back to have a look at me, like only a polar bear can. Slowly, I backed into the cabin and yelled at Bob and Callie to stay where they were. I took up a position at the window to see what the momma bear was going to do. With great relief I watched her head right into the lake with those two little cubs right behind her.

As soon as I thought it was safe, I opened the door and yelled at Bob and Callie to come in. Callie was still in her pajamas but Bob was naked and it was he who came streaking through the cabin with only his towel in front of him.

Momma bear stayed just offshore from the cabin and put on quite a performance for us, diving and rolling over, while her cubs climbed on her back and slid off into the water. When she moved farther out in the lake, we took out the scope and set it up so that we could continue to enjoy them. It was a gorgeous show and at that point, Bob said, "I don't care what the rest of them have done today, they can't possibly have topped this." But then he added, "You can't believe how vulnerable you feel when you are stark naked and there is a nothing but a ¼" piece of chipboard between you and a polar bear!"

Later in the afternoon, the three of us were sitting around reading and waiting for the others to come back when this mental image of Bob, running in holding his towel up in front of him, flitted across my mind. I couldn't help it, I started to giggle. Bob looked up from his book and said, " I know what you are laughing about!"

Simply Salad

When the closest grower for salad greens is 650 miles away you truly appreciate salads. All our fruits and vegetables come through Winnipeg and from there they get to us either by truck to Thompson and then plane to North Knife Lake; or by train to Churchill and then float plane to Dymond Lake. For those of you who are used to running down to the supermarket and picking up the fresh ingredients you need for dinner, this probably sounds like a bit of a nuisance — it is! You have to be able to predict your needs at least four or five days ahead and if something happens and you are shorted in your order or, heaven forbid, the weather is out for a few days, you can get to be quite inventive in the salad and veggie department!

Greek Salad

Everyone has a favorite way to prepare a Greek Salad. We like ours very thinly sliced, not chopped. This is great served with fish, lamb or anything with a tomato sauce. It also makes a great lunch with crusty rolls or French bread.

Greek Dressing:

1 cup	olive oil	250 mL
½ cup	red wine vinegar	125 mL
1 tsp.	salt	5 mL
¼ tsp.	pepper	1 mL
1 tsp.	dried oregano	5 mL
1 tsp.	dried basil	5 mL
2	small garlic cloves, crushed	2
½	red onion, halved and sliced thinly	½
4	large tomatoes, halved and sliced	4
1	English cucumber, halved lengthwise, and sliced	1
1	green pepper, halved and sliced	1
8	leaves romaine lettuce, torn	8
1 cup	pitted black olives, whole OR sliced	250 mL
¾ cup	crumbled feta cheese	175 mL

1. Prepare the dressing first. Shake all the dressing ingredients in a jar or mix with a hand blender.
2. Marinate the sliced red onion in about ½ cup (125 mL) of the dressing while you are preparing the rest of the salad. The longer you let the onions marinate, the milder they will taste.
3. Place the remaining ingredients in a large mixing bowl.
4. Just before serving, add the ½ cup (125 mL) of dressing and the onions to the salad. Toss and add extra dressing if desired. Add only enough dressing to lightly coat the salad ingredients. The rest will keep in a glass jar in the refrigerator for weeks.

Serves 6-8.

See photograph on page 121.

Broccoli Salad

(HELEN) This came to us from my brother-in-law, Gavin. It has become a favorite at both of the lodges. I'm sure Mr. Bush hasn't tried this or he would feel differently about eating his broccoli!

3	large broccoli stems with florets	3
1 lb.	bacon, fried crisp and crumbled	500 g
½ cup	raisins	125 mL
½ cup	sliced almonds OR sunflower seeds	125 mL
1	small red onion, halved, thinly sliced	1

Creamy Cider Dressing:

1 cup	mayonnaise OR similar salad dressing	250 mL
¼ cup	sugar	60 mL
2 tbsp.	cider vinegar	30 mL

1. Peel broccoli stems and cut into bite-sized pieces. Cut up the florets and add to the stems with the bacon, raisins, almonds and red onion.
2. Mix the dressing ingredients together with a whisk.
3. Add the dressing to the broccoli mixture. This keeps well for 1 day.

Serves 6 hungry hunters or 10 grateful guests.

SERVING SUGGESTION: This is great teamed with our Jalapeño Goose, page 20, or on a buffet table, but don't limit its potential. It is great with chicken, fish, beef, pork or whatever.

See photograph on page 17.

Polar Bear Alert

(HELEN) The polar bears were not as numerous when I was growing up in Churchill as they are now. In fact, other than the very odd story, I don't really remember hearing about polar bears until the mid-1960s. As children, we played on the rocks along Hudson Bay without ever giving it a thought. Nowadays the area is posted with polar bear caution signs. When we go down to that area to pick berries we always have someone watching for bears.

On Halloween, the Conservation Officer takes a helicopter tour of the area before dark to see if there are any bears in the area. Then from about 5 p.m. to 9 p.m. both the Natural Resources and Royal Canadian Mounted Police patrol the area to be sure that there are no bear-child encounters.

Those of us who have lived here for many years don't get too excited about it. We just make sure we look both ways — for bears — before crossing the street, or around the corner of a building before charging past. Newcomers have a little trouble with our nonchalant attitude sometimes, but like we tell them, "Hey we haven't had a mugging in Churchill since Jens Munck arrived in 1619!"

Mushroom Bacon Spinach Salad

(HELEN) Susie is the wife of one of our guests and I brought this recipe home after we stopped to visit them in Chicago.

Mustard Wine Dressing:

½ cup	sugar	125 mL
1 tsp.	dry mustard	5 mL
1 tsp.	salt	5 mL
⅓ cup	red wine vinegar	75 mL
1 cup	vegetable oil	250 mL
¼ cup	finely chopped red onion	60 mL
1 tbsp.	celery seed	15 mL
10 oz.	pkg. fresh spinach	283 g
4	hard-boiled eggs, grated	4
1 cup	sliced fresh mushrooms	250 mL
½	medium red onion, thinly sliced	½
8	slices bacon, cooked, crumbled	8

1. Combine sugar, dry mustard, salt and red wine vinegar in a blender for about 30 seconds.
2. Add the oil while running the blender on slow.
3. Stop the blender and add the onion and celery seed; give the blender a 15-second pulse. (This can also be done with a hand blender.)
4. Set aside until you are ready to toss the salad. This is another dressing that keeps well so just put any extra in your refrigerator. It is great with fruit too.
5. Toss the salad ingredients with the dressing in a large bowl, just before serving. Transfer to your serving bowl.

Serves 6-8.

For food in a world where many walk in hunger,
For faith in a world where many walk in fear,
For friends in a world where many walk alone,
We give you humble thanks, O Lord.

Marie's Caesar Salad
Par Excellence!!!

The biggest problem we have with this salad is making sure there is some left for us to eat when the guests are done. At Dymond Lake this fall we resorted to using a five-gallon pail to crisp our romaine and finally there was some left for us. Be sure to try the croûtons. They are well worth the extra work.

1	egg, coddled (put in boiling water for just 1 minute)	1
1	garlic clove, crushed	1
2 tbsp.	lemon juice	30 mL
¼ tsp.	dry mustard	1 mL
½ tsp.	salt	2 mL
⅛ tsp.	pepper	0.5 mL
1 tsp.	Worcestershire sauce	5 mL
¼ cup	olive oil	60 mL
1	head romaine lettuce*	1
⅓ cup	Parmesan cheese	75 mL
1 cup	croûtons**	250 mL
6	slices bacon, cooked, crumbled (optional)	6

1. To make the dressing, blend the first 8 ingredients. (We use a hand blender for this.) This can be done early in the day; just refrigerate until you are ready to use it.
2. Tear romaine lettuce into bite-sized pieces and place in a large bowl.
3. JUST BEFORE SERVING, toss with Parmesan cheese, croûtons, bacon and dressing. Transfer to a serving bowl and serve.

Serves 6.

SERVING SUGGESTIONS: We serve this with our Dynamite Lasagne, page 145, and crusty French bread. It is good with almost any main dish.

* *To crisp romaine lettuce, cut off the stem end, wash it well, shake off the excess water and then pack it either in a plastic zip-lock bag or a refrigerator container with a tight-fitting lid. Throw it in the refrigerator for a couple of hours and it will be nice and crisp!*

** *See Jeanne's Croûtons on page 72.*

Len's Caesar Salad Dressing

(HELEN) Len is one of Doug's brothers. Len used to come out to North Knife to help us with construction and various other projects — until I discovered that he was into gourmet cooking! Now we keep him in the kitchen! This is one of his specialties. It is heavier on the garlic than Marie's so just pick the one that suits your taste buds.

2	anchovies, minced	2
2 tbsp.	lemon juice or juice of ½ a lemon	30 mL
2	garlic cloves, crushed	2
1 tbsp.	Dijon mustard	15 mL
1	egg yolk	1
¼ cup	vegetable oil OR olive oil	60 mL
½ tsp.	Worcestershire sauce	2 mL
3 tbsp.	mayonnaise	45 mL
½ tsp.	salt	2 mL
	freshly ground pepper to taste	
1	head romaine lettuce*	1
½ cup	freshly ground Parmesan cheese	125 mL
½ cup	Caesar croûtons or Jeanne's homemade, page 72	125 mL

1. Blend or shake well the first 9 ingredients. We use a hand blender for this and it works very well. A regular blender or even a jar with a tight fitting lid will work just fine.
2. JUST BEFORE SERVING, toss the dressing with the romaine lettuce, Parmesan cheese and the croûtons.

Serves 6.

* *To crisp romaine lettuce, cut off the stem end, wash it well, shake off the excess water and then pack it either in a plastic zip-lock bag or a refrigerator container with a tight-fitting lid. Throw it in the refrigerator for a couple of hours and it will be nice and crisp!*

Nothing grows faster than a fish from the time he bites until he gets away.

Pepper and Sugar Pea Salad

This is another of Marie's salad concoctions. It is simple, yet very elegant.

> lettuce of your choice
> sliced carrots
> green and red pepper strips
> sliced celery
> fresh sugar OR snow pea pods, cut in half
> tomato wedges
> Herb and Garlic Dressing, below, OR Golden
>   Caesar dressing

1. Just toss the prepared vegetables with Herb and Garlic or Golden Caesar dressing. Go easy on the dressing, you can always add more.

VARIATION: Brother-in-law Len adds yellow pepper and cantaloupe to the above vegetables and tosses it with Golden Italian for another great variation.

See photograph on page 69.

Herb and Garlic Dressing

1 cup	olive oil	250 mL
1/3 cup	red wine vinegar	75 mL
2 tsp.	DLS*	10 mL
1/2 tsp.	salt	2 mL
1 tbsp.	sugar	15 mL
2	garlic cloves, crushed	2

1. Combine all ingredients and mix well.

Makes approximately 1 1/3 cups (325 mL) of dressing.

* *For Dymond Lake Seasoning, substitute 1/2 tsp. (2 mL) each thyme, basil, oregano, marjoram and seasoned pepper. Increase salt to 1 tsp. (5 mL).*

Cucumber Sour Cream Salad

This is a scrumptious and different side dish.

1 tbsp.	sugar	15 mL
1 1/2 tsp.	salt	7 mL
1 cup	sour cream	250 mL
3 tbsp.	grated onion	45 mL
2 tbsp.	white vinegar OR lemon juice	30 mL
4 1/2 cups	thinly sliced cucumbers	1.125 L

1. In a large bowl, combine sugar, salt, sour cream, onion and vinegar.
2. Add cucumbers and mix well. Cover and chill for at least 2 hours.

Serves 8.

Mandarin Orange Salad

When you're in a hurry, here is a simple but impressive salad .

Sweet Mustard Dressing:

½ cup	sugar	125 mL
¼ cup	vinegar	60 mL
1 cup	vegetable oil	250 mL
1 tsp.	salt	5 mL
½	small red onion, chopped	½
1 tsp.	dry mustard	5 mL
2 tbsp.	water	30 mL
1	head romaine lettuce	1
10 oz.	can mandarin orange segments	284 mL
½ cup	slivered almonds OR pecans (toasted OR plain)	125 mL

1. Blend sugar, vinegar, oil, salt, onion, dry mustard and water in your blender until well mixed. (We use the hand blender for this job too.) Make this ahead and refrigerate for a few hours to blend the flavors.
2. Tear lettuce into bite-sized pieces and put into a salad bowl.
3. JUST BEFORE SERVING, add the oranges and nuts and toss with enough dressing to coat the leaves. You will probably have some dressing left over. It keeps well in a covered glass jar in the refrigerator.

Serves 6.

VARIATION: I've made this with fresh strawberries instead of oranges. Yummy!

An enthusiastic angler was telling some friends about a proposed fishing trip to a lake in Canada.

"Are there any trout up there?" asked one friend.

"Thousands of them," replied the angler.

"Will they bite easily?" asked the friend.

"Will they? Why, they're absolutely vicious. A man has to hide behind a tree to bait his hook. The trout are twelve inches."

"That's not very big."

"It is when it's between the eyes. I caught one that was so big the picture of it weighed three pounds."

Fish

Mike's Beer Batter Fish, page 30
Parmesan Potatoes, page 129
Red River Bread, page 41

Mustard Dill Sauce, page 34
Greek Salad, page 114

Onion Salad

(HELEN) My mother-in-law, Jeanne, gave me this recipe before the dawn of time. Actually it was only about 25 years ago. She acquired it when she worked for Gulf Oil. They put on a big company barbecue every year and served Onion Salad.

6	Spanish onions*, very thinly sliced	6
½ cup	vinegar	125 mL
½ cup	water	125 mL
¾ cup	sugar	175 mL
2 tsp.	salt	10 mL
1¼ cups	mayonnaise OR similar salad dressing	300 mL
2 tbsp.	celery seed	30 mL

1. Slice the onions very thinly and place them in a plastic or glass dish.
2. Combine the vinegar, water, sugar and salt. Mix well to dissolve the sugar and salt. Pour over the onions and mix well. Put a plate on top of the onions and set a weight on it. A plastic bottle of oil or vinegar works well. Let the onions sit on the counter all day — overnight is best.
3. Drain the onions. (You will wonder where all the liquid came from!)
4. Combine the dressing and celery seed and toss with the onions. Put into a serving bowl and serve.

Serves 16-20.

SERVING SUGGESTION: This is great served with beef or Jalapeño Goose, page 20. If there is any left over, pile it on a bun with beef or goose the next day for a super lunch!

* *We often don't have Spanish onions, so will use whatever is at hand. It is best if they aren't too strong, but the sportsmen love them anyway. Strong onions can be toned down quickly by pouring hot water over the slices (especially if they have been separated into rings), allowed to sit for a while (5 minutes will do) and drained — before continuing with the marinade.*

See photograph on page 17.

Dymond Lake Lodge –

Located on the shores of Hudson Bay, Dymond Lake is the first waterfowl hunting lodge on the central flyway.

Creamy Green Coleslaw with Elaine's Dressing

Elaine is the wife of Len, the carpenter who built North Knife Lake Lodge. He is a carpenter by trade but anyone who has seen the lodge knows that he is really an artist at heart. Elaine and their two daughters accompanied him on some of his trips to the lodge and Elaine, brought recipes with her. A number of them have become regulars at both lodges.

6 cups	grated cabbage	1.5 L
1 cup	finely chopped green pepper	250 mL
½ cup	finely chopped celery	125 mL
¼ cup	finely chopped green onion	60 mL
½ cup	vegetable oil	125 mL
½ cup	vinegar	125 mL
¼ cup	mayonnaise OR similar salad dressing	60 mL
¼ cup	sugar	60 mL
1 tsp.	salt	5 mL

1. Combine the cabbage, green pepper, celery and green onion in bowl.
2. Mix oil, vinegar, mayonnaise, sugar and salt and add to the cabbage mixture.

Serves 8.

Old-Fashioned Salad Dressing

(MARIE) Not many of us make our own salad dressing these days, but I grew up on this one. It has a much richer vinegar taste than the manufactured variety. It's good for dipping vegetables or on a potato salad.

⅓ cup	flour	75 mL
2 tsp.	dry mustard	10 mL
1 tsp.	salt	5 mL
½ cup	sugar	125 mL
1 cup	water	250 mL
4	eggs	4
1 cup	vinegar	250 mL
2 tsp.	butter OR margarine (optional)	10 mL

1. Blend together the first 7 ingredients, adding vinegar last.
2. Cook and stir over medium heat until the dressing thickens. Add butter if desired.
3. Store in a glass jar in the refrigerator. It keeps indefinitely.

Makes 1 quart (1 L) of dressing.

Vegging Out

Fresh vegetables are of prime importance in all of our meals at the Lodges. As we have mentioned, fruits and vegetables are our trickiest commodity to obtain and keep on hand. As soon as the airplane arrives, the veggies are rushed up to the Lodges and into the coolers. We don't want to traumatize them any further! We've added some great grain recipes to this section also. Wild and tame rice dishes complement any meal.

Marie's Wild Rice Casserole Suprême

We have found more complicated recipes for a wild rice casserole than this, but we have never found one that brings us more rave reviews. We try to make enough to ensure that we have leftovers for Cream of Wild Rice Soup, page 71.

1 cup	uncooked whole kernel wild rice	250 mL
3 cups	beef broth	750 mL
¼ tsp.	thyme	1 mL
¼ tsp.	basil	1 mL
½ cup	butter OR margarine	125 mL
⅓ cup	finely chopped onions	75 mL
½ lb.	fresh mushrooms, sliced, OR 10 oz. (284 mL) can	250 g
½ cup	evaporated milk OR light cream	125 mL

1. Rinse wild rice with cold water and place in a large pot with the beef broth, thyme and basil. Bring to a boil, cover and simmer for 1 hour, or until tender. Remove from the heat and let sit for 30 minutes to absorb the remaining liquid.
2. Melt the butter in a large frying pan. Add the onions, and sauté until translucent. Add the mushrooms and brown lightly.
3. Combine the rice, mushroom, onion mixture and evaporated milk. Place in a greased 1½-quart (1.5 L) casserole.
4. Bake in a 350°F (180°C) oven for 30 minutes, until heated through.

Serves 6.

SERVING SUGGESTIONS: Served with Jalapeño Goose Breasts, page 20, or Honey Garlic Cornish Game Hens, page 153, this dish is a sure winner. It's dynamite combined with Mushroom Goose, page 22, and fresh Cranberry Sauce, page 198. The textures and flavor combinations complement each other perfectly!

TIME-SAVING TIP: You can make this a day or 2 ahead and refrigerate it. Just increase the oven time by 15 minutes. It even freezes well, so double the recipe and freeze a batch for another day.

COOKING TIP: Cooking time for wild rice varies according to how the rice has been parched (dried).

See photograph on page 17.

Oven-Fried Rice

This is one of those "throw it in the oven and forget about it" recipes that we love. It leaves you free to do all sorts of last minute tasks.

2 cups	long-grain rice	500 mL
1½ oz.	onion soup mix (1 pkg.)	40 g
½ cup	vegetable oil	125 mL
¼ cup	soy sauce	60 mL
	boiling water	
10 oz.	can sliced mushrooms	284 mL
3	green onions, chopped	3

1. Pour the rice into a 2-quart (2 L) greased casserole or a 9 x 13" (23 x 33 cm) pan.
2. In a large bowl or 4-cup (1 L) measuring cup, combine the onion soup mix, oil and soy sauce. Add enough boiling water to make 4 cups (1 L).
3. Pour the liquid over the rice, add the mushrooms and green onions and stir lightly with a fork.
4. Cover and bake at 350°F (180°C) for 1 hour.

Serves 8.

SERVING SUGGESTION: This dish teams up well with chicken or ribs.

COOKING TIP: We double and triple this recipe at the Lodges. The secret is to add ½ cup (125 mL) of water and an additional 15 minutes cooking time per recipe.

Old McWebber had a Farm

(HELEN) Doug calls himself a lodge operator but we suspect there is a bit of farmer in him too. The following are some of his extra projects for North Knife Lake.

We have a cold frame in which we grow strawberries, we have a number of raspberry, rhubarb and chive patches. We grow our own mint, dill, lemon balm and other assorted herbs. He is getting very serious about this and now has the material to put up a 50-foot greenhouse in which we will try to grow a variety of fruits and vegetables for the lodge. He has had us composting for years already, in fact you need a two-hour training session just to handle the garbage in the kitchen. There is a pail for compost, a pail for chicken feed (yes we keep laying chickens), a pail for coffee and tea water (for watering), a garbage bin for nonburnables (which we fly out), a bin for burnables, a bag for returnable pop cans, a bag for returnable beer cans and who knows what new ones he will have for this year.

We tease him about all this but when you combine his composting and recycling with our Solar/Battery system for electricity at the lodge we have a very ecologically friendly plant that we are very proud of. I am not too sure if I am going to go for the worm farm he keeps threatening to get! He also wants a couple of pigs and I keep telling him he can certainly have pigs if he wants them, he just can't have pigs and me at the same time at North Knife Lake. So far, I am winning!

Len's Herbed and Spiced Oven-Roasted Potatoes

(HELEN) This is an easy but elegant addition to a nice roast lamb or beef dinner. Len introduced us to it the first time that a group of McDonald's personnel came to fish with us at North Knife Lake.

8	large potatoes, peeled and halved OR quartered lengthwise	8
½ cup	vegetable oil	125 mL
1 tbsp.	DLS*	15 mL
2	garlic cloves, crushed	2

1. Dry the peeled potatoes thoroughly after washing. We use a clean terry towel for this purpose because we do not advocate the use of paper towels.
2. Pour the vegetable oil into a shallow roasting or baking pan. Stir in the DLS* and crushed garlic cloves. Add the potatoes and use a pastry brush to coat them with oil from the bottom of the pan.
3. Place the pan of potatoes in a 400°F (200°C) oven and roast for 45-60 minutes, turning at least twice. When finished, the potatoes should be crispy and brown.

Serves 6-8.

COOKING TIP: If you are cooking a roast at the same time at a lower temperature and only have 1 oven, allow about 15 extra minutes for cooking the potatoes and put them in at the same temperature as the roast. When you take the roast out to let it sit for 15 or 20 minutes before carving, crank the oven up to 425°F (220°C) to crisp the potatoes!

* *For Dymond Lake Seasoning, substitute 1 tsp. (5 mL) seasoned salt, ½ tsp. (2 mL) seasoned pepper, ¼ tsp. (1 mL) thyme leaves, ½ tsp. (2 mL) parsley, ¼ tsp. (1 mL) basil.*

See photograph on page 155.

> **Blessed be Thou Lord God of the universe**
> **Who bringest forth bread from the earth**
> **and makest glad the heart of men**
> **An ancient Hebrew prayer**

  *Vegging Out*

Parmesan Potatoes

These are so simple and sooo good!

½ cup	margarine	125 mL
½ cup	flour	125 mL
½ cup	Parmesan cheese	125 mL
2 tsp.	DLS* OR 1 tsp. (5 mL) salt and ½ tsp. (2 mL) pepper	10 mL
10	large potatoes, peeled and cut into pieces the size of a small egg	10

1. Put the margarine on a baking pan with raised sides and place it in a 375°F (190°C) oven to melt the margarine.
2. Mix the flour, Parmesan and DLS* in a heavy plastic bag.
3. Shake the potato pieces in the flour mixture and place in the melted margarine on the baking sheet.
4. Return the pan to the hot oven and bake for 1 hour and 15 minutes, turning the potatoes every 15 minutes so they get crispy and golden brown.

Serves 8 men or 10 women. For smaller numbers, reduce all ingredients by half.

SERVING SUGGESTION: These are great with Beer Batter Fish, page 30, Crispy Fried Fish, page 28, or Crispy Oven-Fried Chicken, page 160, and Creamy Green Coleslaw, page 124, fresh corn on the cob if it's in season (or kernel corn if it's not) and Crusty Rolls, page 40. Finish it off with a nice Nectarine Roll, page 166, and you have a feast fit for a royalty!

* *Dymond Lake Seasoning*

See photograph on page 121.

*The fishing was so bad on our vacation
that even the liars didn't catch any.*

Heavenly Hash Browns

Mike Boll, our head guide, told me that we could feed him these for dinner every night and he wouldn't complain. It is also Tina's favorite (Marie's daughter) and she isn't as easy to please as Mike! Make this ahead, then put it in the oven and forget about it while you whip up some fancy taste teasers or luscious desserts!

2 lbs.	frozen hash-brown potatoes, slightly thawed	1 kg
2 x 10 oz.	cans cream of mushroom soup	2 x 284 mL
½ cup	melted butter OR margarine	125 mL
2 cups	sour cream	500 mL
½ cup	grated onion	125 mL
½ tsp.	salt	2 mL
¼ tsp.	pepper	1 mL
2 cups	grated Cheddar cheese	500 mL
	Parmesan Cheese	

1. In a very large bowl, mix together the hash browns, soup, butter, sour cream, onion, salt, pepper and Cheddar cheese.
2. Pour into a 9 x 13" (23 x 33 cm) baking dish and sprinkle with Parmesan cheese.
3. Bake at 350°F (180°C) for 1¼-1½ hours, until set and the top is golden brown.

Serves 6 hunting or fishing guides or 10 ordinary people!

VARIATION: When caught without frozen hash browns, we cook our own diced potatoes. They must be totally cooked. Decrease the amount of sour cream by ½ cup (125 mL) and the melted butter by ¼ cup (60 mL).

For food we eat, and those who prepare it,
For health to enjoy it and friends to share it.
We thank thee O Lord.
                    Bishop Kenneth Lamplugh

Creamy Oven-Mashed Potatoes

(HELEN) This recipe has become one of our family favorites. I especially like this dish because you can make it ahead of time and either refrigerate or freeze it — just pop it in the oven when you need it. That is a real plus when you are trying to take care of all the last minute dinner details, like carving meat and making gravy.

5 lbs.	potatoes, peeled and quartered	2.2 kg
8 oz.	cream cheese, at room temperature	250 g
1 cup	sour cream	250 mL
2 tsp.	onion salt	10 mL
1 tsp.	salt	5 mL
¼ tsp.	pepper	1 mL
2 tbsp.	butter OR regular margarine	30 mL

1. Cook the potatoes in boiling salted water until tender. Drain well.
2. Mash the potatoes with a potato masher until smooth. Add the cream cheese, sour cream, onion salt, salt and pepper. Beat with a wire whisk or electric beaters until smooth and fluffy.
3. Place potatoes in a greased 2-quart (2 L) casserole, dot them with butter, cover and heat at 350°F (180°C) for 45 minutes, or until heated through. OR place potatoes in a freezer-proof dish. Allow them to cool and then cover them. Either freeze or refrigerate. They will keep in the refrigerator for about 1 week and in the freezer for up to 3 months. Ensure they are completely thawed before heating, or add at least 15 minutes to the cooking time.

Serves 10-12. This recipe makes about 8 cups (2 L); if using them for a small group you can freeze half the potatoes to use another day.

SERVING SUGGESTION: If you are serving these potatoes with an entrée that does not have gravy, remove the lid and top the casserole with a layer of grated cheese for the last 15 minutes of baking.

God, may we eat all we are able
Until our stomachs touch the table.

Sweet 'N' Sassy Potatoes

Slightly reminiscent of scalloped potatoes but with a delicious new twist.

18	small new potatoes, unpeeled and halved	18
	OR 10 regular potatoes, peeled and quartered	
⅔ cup	finely chopped onions	150 mL
3 tbsp.	butter OR margarine	45 mL
2 tbsp.	sugar	30 mL
1 tsp.	salt	5 mL
2 tbsp.	flour	30 mL
1½ cups	milk	375 mL
1 cup	sour cream	250 mL
2 tbsp.	white vinegar	30 mL

1. Boil the potatoes until tender but not mushy. Drain and set aside.
2. In a medium-sized saucepan, sauté the onion in butter until translucent. Remove from heat and stir in the sugar, salt and flour. Gradually add milk stirring constantly to keep the mixture smooth. Return to the heat and simmer until thick, stirring constantly. Add sour cream and vinegar. Cook just until the sauce begins to bubble. DO NOT ALLOW TO BOIL.
3. Combine the sauce and potatoes. Serve hot.

Serves 10.

SERVING SUGGESTION: Great with ham or Stuffed Baked Lake Trout, page 32, — let your imagination be your guide.

Zucchini Casserole

This casserole can be layered or mixed. Whichever you do, it is a winning blend of flavors.

1 cup	cubed zucchini	250 mL
1 cup	cubed tomatoes	250 mL
1 cup	chopped onions	250 mL
1 cup	cubed green peppers	250 mL
10 oz.	can sliced or whole mushrooms, drained OR	284 mL
	1 cup (250 mL) fresh mushrooms	
½-1 tbsp.	DLS* OR seasoned salt and seasoned pepper	7-15 mL
	to taste	
1 cup	grated mozzarella cheese	250 mL

Zucchini Casserole

Continued

1. Layer or combine all ingredients, except cheese, in a greased 1½-quart (1.5 L) casserole. Top with grated cheese. (The cheese may be mixed in with the vegetables, if you prefer.)
2. Cover and cook in a 350°F (180°C) oven for 45 minutes; vegetables should be just tender-crisp.

Serves 4-6.

NOTE: This recipe doubles and triples very well, so don't be afraid to use it the next time you have a crowd for dinner. Also, we sometimes mix half Cheddar and half mozzarella cheese.

* *Dymond Lake Seasoning*

Aphrodisiac Green Beans

This recipe is another that Len introduced us to when McDonald's Corporation first came to visit. It truly takes green beans from the earthly realm to the heavenly one.

3 lbs.	green beans	1.5 kg
½ cup	butter	125 mL
3	garlic cloves, crushed (or more to taste)	3
1 tsp.	salt	5 mL
1 cup	slivered almonds	250 mL

1. Wash green beans and halve each one crosswise. BLANCH* them in boiling water. This may be done early in the day; set aside until you are ready to finish cooking them.
2. Melt the butter in a large skillet or wok over medium heat. Add the crushed garlic and well-drained green beans. Sprinkle with salt and continue to stir-fry for 10-12 minutes, until just tender-crisp. Add the almonds; stir-fry for 1 minute.

Serves 8-10.

* *TO BLANCH: Bring a large pot of water to a full boil and add the vegetables. Bring the water back to a boil, immediately remove from the heat and drain; rinse the vegetables with very cold water and drain again.*

See photograph on page 155.

Dilled Carrots

We discovered this one night when we were caught short and didn't want to serve just plain carrots. There really isn't much different about these but the dill adds a pleasing, new dimension to the flavor.

2 cups	sliced carrots	500 mL
¼ cup	butter	60 mL
1 tsp.	dillweed	5 mL
¼ tsp.	salt	1 mL
	dash OR 2 of pepper	

1. Cook the sliced carrots until tender-crisp either by steaming in a pot over a burner or in the microwave. Drain.
2. Stir in the butter, dillweed, salt and pepper.

Serves 4.

Carrots Provençale*

Instead of the dill, salt and pepper, add 1 tsp. (5 mL) of Provençale to the butter. It gives a garlic and parsley flavor.

* *Provençale is a mixture of herbs and spices. You will find it with the other seasonings in your supermarket, see note on page 34.*

Glazed Carrots

Instead of dill, add 2 tbsp. (30 mL) of brown sugar to the butter and toss with the carrots. (I especially like this combo with roast turkey or chicken.)

COOKING TIP: Just another little thought about carrots that Doug's Mother passed along to us — ½ cup (125 mL) of carrots per person is a good rule of thumb. We have found this to be very accurate whether we are feeding 4 or 40.

MOTHER'S HELPER: Marie found that her children preferred their cooked carrots mashed slightly with a potato masher.

Broccoli and/or Cauliflower Au Gratin

(HELEN) Broccoli and cauliflower are a couple of the hardier vegetables we are able to get for the Lodges so we use them a lot. One night, I was a little short of the broccoli and cauliflower so I steamed up some carrots and added them — it was delicious! Be creative — it's fun! We prepare this recipe two different ways, depending on our time: directly from stove to table, or made ahead in a casserole.

1	bunch of broccoli OR a large cauliflower	1
3 tbsp.	butter OR margarine	45 mL
3 tbsp.	flour	45 mL
1 cup	milk	250 mL
1 tsp.	DLS* OR ½ tsp.(2 mL) salt and ¼ tsp. (1 mL) pepper	5 mL
1 cup	grated medium Cheddar cheese	250 mL

1. Wash broccoli and cauliflower, peel broccoli stems and cut into large bite-sized pieces. Steam or microwave until tender-crisp, 5-10 minutes. Drain well and set aside.
2. Melt the butter over low heat in a heavy saucepan until bubbly. Remove the pan from the heat and stir in the flour with a wire whisk or wooden spoon until smooth.
3. Slowly add the milk, a little at a time, stirring constantly to keep it smooth.
4. Add the seasoning and return to a medium heat. Cook, stirring constantly, until the sauce comes to a boil and thickens.
5. Remove the sauce from heat and add the cheese, stirring well until the cheese is melted and smooth. You might want to use a wire whisk for the last bit of milk and cheese.
6. Pour the sauce over the vegetables, stir lightly and serve.

Serves 6.

VARIATION: Place the vegetables in a 1-quart (1 L) casserole and sprinkle with ½ cup (125 mL) of fine bread crumbs mixed with 2 tbsp. (30 mL) of melted butter or margarine. Cover and refrigerate until you are ready to cook. Heat at 350°F (180°C) for 30 minutes before serving.

COOKING TIP: To ensure a smooth cheese sauce, don't let the sauce boil after you have added the cheese.

* *Dymond Lake Seasoning*

Elegant Parmesan Cauliflower

(HELEN) This is so simple and yet so impressive! The recipe came from my friend, Bonnie Chartier, another born and bred Churchillian. Bonnie is our resident professional birder and an authority on the natural history of the Churchill area. She also runs Churchill Wilderness Encounter, a company that takes people out to view POLAR BEARS. In fact, Bonnie and I have had a few bear encounters of our own!*

1	large head of cauliflower, trimmed but whole	1
¼ cup	mayonnaise	60 mL
¼ cup	Parmesan cheese	60 mL

1. Either steam or microwave the whole cauliflower head until it is barely tender. Place in a shallow ovenproof dish.
2. Mix the mayonnaise and Parmesan cheese together and spread over the cauliflower.
3. Place the dish in a 350°F (180°C) oven for 15-20 minutes, until the topping is golden brown. Serve it whole. Your guests can just use the serving spoon to cut away their portions.

Serves 6.

* *Read about Bonnie in the story, "North Knife Lake, Where Are Youuuu?" on page 138.*

> *Thank you, God, for rain and sun*
> *And all the plants that grow,*
> *Thank you for our daily food*
> *And friends that love us so.*
> *Inyanga, Zimbabwe*

Peppers and Pasta Alfredo

Served with Veal Marsala, it's dynamite! When Len makes this he slices his vegetables very, very, very thin. We just slice them thin. Your preference rules!

¼	medium onion, finely chopped	¼
1	large garlic clove, crushed	1
½ cup	butter	125 mL
3 tbsp.	flour	45 mL
1 tsp.	DLS* OR ½ tsp. (2 mL) salt, ¼ tsp. (1 mL) pepper	5 mL
¼	yellow pepper, thinly sliced	¼
¼	red pepper, thinly sliced	¼
¼	green pepper, thinly sliced	¼
3	green onions, finely chopped	3
1	celery rib, finely chopped	1
⅔ cup	slivered ham OR bacon	150 mL
2 cups	half & half cream (10% m.f.)	500 mL
⅔ cup	grated Parmesan cheese	150 mL
4 cups	cooked pasta of your choice*	1 L

1. Sauté the onion and garlic in butter, until the onions are soft and translucent. Add the flour and seasoning. Stir and cook for about 2 minutes.
2. Add the peppers, green onions, celery and ham or bacon. Cook for a couple of minutes and then add the cream. Bring to a boil.
3. Add the Parmesan and simmer for a few minutes.
4. Stir your favorite pasta into the sauce and let the pasta absorb the sauce flavors for a few minutes before serving.

Serves 4-6.

NOTE: The usual recommended pasta serving is 1 lb. (500 g) for 4 people — maybe more for fishermen and hunters.

* *We use fettuccine, linguine or medium egg noodles.*

"North Knife Lake, Where Are Youuuu?"

We had just moved over from Dymond Lake to North Knife to work on the fishing segment of the Guide Training Course. Trapper Don was out on the lake with the twenty students so they could practice their fish guiding and shore lunch techniques. Bonnie was back at the lodge with me and, you guessed it, I was in the kitchen, where there were fresh rolls, cinnamon buns, cakes and cookies all cooling on the counter. It was a beautiful afternoon, the sun was shining and, since the students were cooking their dinner out on the lake, I had some free time.

Bonnie suggested we take a hike along the esker and look for berries; I thought that was a wonderful idea, so off we went with our bug jackets and berry bowls. Oh yes, and Bonnie brought along her pistol just in case we ran into any unfriendly black bears. Well, we had only been gone about half an hour and the berries were proving to be a little under ripe for picking. I thought it might be an idea to head back to camp to catch a little nap since we had been short of sleep. Bonnie concurred so we turned around (so we thought) and headed back to camp. We walked and we walked and we walked some more. Nothing looked familiar at all. The bush was getting thicker and the bugs were getting buggier and there was no lake to be seen anywhere! I said, " Okay Bonnie, you are the naturalist here, where are we and how do we get back to camp?" Her answer was anything but helpful. She said, "I've been looking down checking out the plants and critters. This is your territory — I thought you knew the way."

Well, to make a long day into a short story, it took us another five hours to finally find the lake. I was afraid of heights and had never climbed a tree in my life; that day I climbed three trying to find the lake. I tried to convince Bonnie that she should do the climbing but she said that, since she was bigger than I was, it was her job to stand at the bottom to catch me if I fell. (I really think that she was as afraid of heights as I was.) Anyway, she stood at the bottom and urged me to just go up one more branch. She was also very encouraging when we were in the middle of a big bog. (We had already gone around it once in our frenzied wanderings and I was too tired to go around again.) So, there we were in the middle when she very quietly said "Helen, try to keep your weight spread out as much as possible, this is one of those bogs that if we break through we will likely just keep on going." And she thought I had to know that right then! With a little help from a floatplane, that we were fortunate enough to see land, we did finally find the lake but we were now a good mile south of the lodge. We started walking along the shore to the lodge when we heard a boat coming. It turned out that when our friend, Ike, landed in the floatplane, and found the place deserted he decided something was not right. He took off and found the guides on the lake. A couple of them thought they had better come back and see what was up. Now that pistol that Bonnie had been hauling around all day, and holding over her head in the bog so it wouldn't get wet finally came to some use. She fired it into the air and got the boat's attention so they came over to investigate. They seemed to find the sight of Bonnie and me looking very sunburned, soaking wet and totally exhausted very funny. They did take pity on us though and gave us a ride back to camp.

So, if you should come to visit us at North Knife, you will probably notice orange tape tied on a number of the trees. Like the American Express Ad says, "Don't leave home without it, when going for a walk in the bush!"

Vegging Out

Tame Meats To Make You Wild

As well as recipes for wild meat that give a whole new meaning to the term "wild meal", we have some recipes for tame meats that will get you some wild reviews. Again , these are all recipes that we use at the Lodges so they have had a lot of "field testing". As you can see, we serve entrées that run the spectrum from " very elegant" to the " stick-to-your-ribs" variety.

Prime Rib with Mushrooms Au Jus

Many cooks are intimidated at the thought of cooking a prime rib but it is really very simple and yet such an elegant meal to serve.

8-10 lb.	prime rib roast (or standing rib as it is sometimes called) DLS*	3.5-4.5 kg
3	garlic cloves, crushed	3

1. Bring the roast to room temperature before proceeding and preheat the oven to 425°F (220°C).
2. Place the roast, fat side up, in a large heavy roasting pan. Rub crushed garlic all over the top and sides.
3. Sprinkle the roast very liberally (at least 2 tbsp. [30 mL]) with DLS*. The top of the roast should be well covered with spices.
4. Roast, UNCOVERED, for 15 minutes at 425°F (220°C). Reduce the temperature to 325°F (160°C) and continue to roast 20 minutes per pound for rare, 25 minutes per pound for medium and 30 minutes per pound for well.
5. Remove the roast from the roaster and let it rest for 10 minutes before carving. While it is resting, prepare the Mushroom Au Jus, below.

Serves 10-12.

SERVING SUGGESTION: We often serve this with either baked or Len's Herbed and Spiced Oven-Roasted Potatoes, page 128, Aphrodisiac Green Beans, page 133, and Yorkshire Pudding, page 55. Add a Caesar, page 117 or 118, or green salad and top it off with a selection from our desserts!

* *For Dymond Lake Seasoning substitute seasoned salt, seasoned pepper, parsley, thyme and celery salt.*

Mushrooms Au Jus

1½ oz.	pkg. onion soup mix	40 g
10 oz.	can beef consommé	284 mL
10 oz.	can sliced mushrooms, undrained	284 mL
2 cups	water	500 mL

1. Skim the grease from the roasting pan as best you can. It doesn't hurt to leave some behind.
2. To the roaster add the onion soup mix, beef consommé, mushrooms with liquid and the water. Simmer on low while you carve the roast.

SERVING SUGGESTION: Serve in a gravy boat. Pour it over prime rib and Yorkshire Pudding. It will pool on your plate and add great flavor to your potatoes and vegetables too!

Tame Meats

Len's Steak with Seasoned Butter

(HELEN) Here's that brother-in-law, Len, again. This is a great alternative to grilling steaks with barbecue sauce. Just as good, very easy and very Gourmet! Make the seasoned butter ahead, and keep it in the freezer.

1¼-1½" (3-4 cm) steaks to feed the crew
 (rib eye OR tenderloin are best)
vegetable oil
fresh garlic cloves, crushed
DLS* OR seasoned salt and seasoned pepper

1. Put the steaks in a dish and pour oil over (about ¼ cup [60 mL] for every 4 steaks).
2. Crush a couple of garlic cloves over the steaks and sprinkle liberally with seasonings.
3. Let steaks marinate for 4-6 hours. Bring steaks to room temperature before cooking.
4. Cook steaks on the barbecue until they are done the way everybody likes them. Serve with a pat of Seasoned Butter, below, on each steak.

Seasoned Butter

1 tbsp.	vegetable oil	15 mL
1	shallot OR small onion	1
3	garlic cloves, crushed	3
1 tbsp.	finely chopped capers	15 mL
½ tsp.	dried tarragon leaves (scant)	2 mL
2 tsp.	Dijon mustard	10 mL
2 tsp.	balsamic OR red wine vinegar	10 mL
2 tsp.	Worcestershire sauce	10 mL
½ tsp.	DLS* OR seasoned pepper	2 mL
1 tsp.	dried parsley	5 mL
½ lb.	butter, softened	250 g

1. In a frying pan, heat oil; sauté shallots, garlic, capers and tarragon leaves until shallots are soft.
2. Remove from the heat and add the mustard, vinegar, Worcestershire, DLS* and parsley. Cool.
3. Beat the cooled garlic mixture into the butter. Chill until stiff enough to handle. Form into a roll and wrap in waxed paper. Refrigerate if you are going to use it the same day. Put in a plastic bag and freeze if you are going to keep it for any length of time.

Makes about 1 cup (250 mL) of seasoned butter.

* *Dymond Lake Seasoning*

French Steak

This is one of those recipes with an unusual combination of ingredients that blend well together. It is different and delicious.

2 lbs.	round steak, cut in serving-sized pieces	1 kg
	flour	
	salt and pepper OR DLS* to taste	
2 tbsp.	butter OR margarine	30 mL
2 tbsp.	olive oil	30 mL
2	large onions, thinly sliced	2
1	garlic clove, crushed	1
1 cup	white wine	250 mL
1 cup	beef bouillon	250 mL
1 tsp.	Worcestershire sauce	5 mL
1 tsp.	soy sauce	5 mL
¼ tsp.	pepper	1 mL
1 cup	grated Cheddar cheese	250 mL
½ cup	sour cream OR yogurt	125 mL

1. Dredge the steak in flour and spices and brown it in a frying pan with the butter and oil. Set steak aside.
2. Add the onions to the frying pan and sauté until golden. Stir in garlic, wine, bouillon, Worcestershire, soy sauce and pepper, being sure to include all the brown bits from the bottom of the pan.
3. Return the steak to the pan, cover and simmer for 1½ hours, or until the meat is very tender. Remove the meat to a platter and keep warm. (I usually pop this in the oven at 325°F (160°C) for 2½ hours rather than doing it on the stove. You can do it either way.)
4. Stir the cheese into the pan juices until melted. Add the sour cream and heat but DO NOT BOIL.
5. Pour the sauce over the meat and serve.

Serves 4-6.

SERVING SUGGESTIONS: This is good with baked potatoes or Len's Herbed and Spiced Oven-Roasted Potatoes, page 128.

* *Dymond Lake Seasoning*

Beef Burgundy

(HELEN) This is a recipe that I found early in our marriage and it is still a family favorite. We serve it at the lodge with many compliments although I was a little upset when one guest said, "This is mighty good stew." Oh well, as long as he liked it I really shouldn't complain. We often substitute moose or caribou for the beef so don't be afraid to experiment.

6	slices bacon	6
2 lbs.	boneless chuck beef roast	1 kg
¼ cup	flour	60 mL
1 tsp.	DLS* OR salt and pepper	5 mL
2	garlic cloves, crushed	2
¾ cup	chopped onion	175 mL
1 cup	red Burgundy wine	250 mL
1 cup	beef consommé	250 mL
1	beef bouillon cube (1 tsp. [5 mL])	1
2	bay leaves	2
¼ tsp.	dried thyme	1 mL
⅛ tsp.	ground cloves	0.5 mL
½ cup	sliced fresh mushrooms OR 10 oz. (284 mL) can sliced mushrooms	125 mL

1. Pan-fry bacon until crisp, remove from the frying pan and set aside.
2. Cut the beef in bite-sized pieces. Dredge in flour seasoned with the DLS* or salt and pepper. Brown in bacon drippings in the frying pan. Remove to a Dutch oven.
3. To the frying pan, add garlic and onions and brown slightly. Add to the beef in the Dutch oven. Add the wine, consommé, bouillon, bay leaves, thyme and cloves. Cover and simmer for 1½-2 hours.
4. Fifteen minutes before the beef is cooked, add the mushrooms and remove the bay leaves.
5. Spoon the beef into a serving dish and crumble the bacon over the top.

Serves 6.

SERVING SUGGESTION: This is great served with rice or noodles.

* *Dymond Lake Seasoning*

Dymond Lake Spaghetti Sauce

(HELEN) 23 years ago, Doug worked as a firefighter for 1 year and brought this recipe home with him from the job.

3 lbs.	ground beef	1.5 kg
1½ cups	chopped onion	375 mL
½ cup	chopped celery	125 mL
2 x 13 oz.	cans tomato paste	2 x 369 mL
48 oz.	can tomato juice	1.36 L
2 tbsp.	dried basil	30 mL
2 tbsp.	dried oregano	30 mL
3	garlic cloves, minced, OR 1 tsp. (5 mL) garlic powder	3
1 tbsp.	DLS* OR salt and pepper to taste	15 mL
2 tbsp.	Tabasco sauce	30 mL
¼ cup	sugar	60 mL
⅔ cup	vinegar	150 mL
2 tsp.	Worcestershire sauce	10 mL
2	bay leaves	2
2 dashes	allspice	2 dashes

1. In a frying pan, brown the hamburger with the onions and celery. Drain and put into a large heavy pot.
2. Add the rest of the ingredients and simmer for at least 2 hours — 4 hours is even better. Be sure to stir occasionally so that it doesn't stick.

Makes 5 quarts (5 L) of sauce.

NOTE: You can substitute 3 x 28 oz. (3 x 796 mL) cans blended tomatoes (we just blend our own) for the tomato juice. Add MORE or LESS juice OR tomatoes to obtain the desired sauce consistency.

Freeze any leftovers in desired amounts for lasagne, pizza, etc.

Shari's Hot Version

That was Doug's version, now here is our daughter Shari's hot . . . version. Make the spaghetti sauce just as described above but add:

1 tbsp.	tamoline**	15 mL
1 tbsp.	chili powder (hot if you have it)	15 mL
2 tbsp.	DLS*	30 mL

If this still isn't hot enough, just pass a bowl of jalapeños!

SERVING SUGGESTION: This sauce is great served over your favorite pasta or turn the page for our Dynamite Lasagne Recipe.

* *Dymond Lake Seasoning*
** *Tamoline — hot chili powder or cayenne*

Tame Meats

Dynamite Lasagne

What makes this lasagne special is the sauce. If exploding taste buds are your craving, use Shari's HOT version of Dymond Lake Spaghetti Sauce, page 144.

7 cups	Dymond Lake Spaghetti Sauce, page 144	1.75 L
16	oven-ready lasagne noodles	16
	Parmesan cheese	
2 cups	cottage cheese	500 mL
1	egg	1
½ cup	Parmesan cheese	125 mL
1 cup	grated medium Cheddar cheese	250 mL
1 cup	grated mozzarella cheese	250 mL

1. Spread a thin layer of spaghetti sauce (approximately 1 cup [250 mL]) in the bottom of a 9 x 13" (23 x 33 cm) pan. Cover with a layer of noodles. We lay 3 the long way and break 1 off to lay across the end.
2. Combine the cottage cheese, egg and Parmesan cheese and spread over the lasagne noodles. Cover with another layer of lasagne noodles.
3. Cover with another layer of sauce, (approximately 2 cups [500 mL]) sprinkle with Parmesan cheese, cover with another layer of noodles, 2 cups (500 mL) sauce, Parmesan, noodles and then 2 cups (500 mL) sauce. (You should have 4 layers of noodles at this point.)
4. Sprinkle with the Cheddar and mozzarella cheeses.
5. Preheat oven to 350°F (180°C). Bake the lasagne, uncovered, for 45 minutes — it should be bubbly hot. Remove lasagne from the oven and let rest for 5 minutes before cutting.

Serves 6-8

SERVING SUGGESTION: Team with Caesar Salad, page 117 or 118, and hot French Bread, page 44, and you have a meal fit for Caesar himself! And for dessert how about Pavlova Nests from "Up Over", page 189.

A Little "Seasoned" Humor

One day towards the end of the season, Helen was attempting to use up all the meat that was left in the freezer. She found a frozen lump of ground meat that Doug had obviously placed there last winter after moose hunting — she probably hadn't noticed it before because the freezer was too full. It would do just fine for our hot and spicy Lasagne sauce. Sure enough, everyone asked for seconds, as usual.

A few days later, Doug came looking for the black bear meat he had left in the freezer. Why did Doug have bear meat in the freezer? Who knows? But it was far too late to have a queasy stomach now. Besides, who was going to tell? Not me! No, we are not going to reveal the year of this gag (pun intended). But we will guarantee that it won't happen again!

Tame Meats **145**

Len's Veal with Marsala Sauce

When the McDonald's crew visited North Knife Lake, we went all out to please them. As Idgie said, in the movie Fried Green Tomatoes, "The secret's in the sauce." We know you'll agree.

¼ cup	butter	60 mL
3	green onions, finely sliced	3
2	garlic cloves, crushed	2
¼ lb.	mushrooms, sliced	125 g
1 tbsp.	flour	15 mL
½ cup	Marsala OR Madeira wine	125 mL
½ cup	beef consommé (canned is best)	125 mL
¼ tsp.	onion salt	1 mL
½ tsp.	DLS* OR seasoned pepper	2 mL
6	veal cutlets, lightly breaded	6
	butter	

1. Melt the ¼ cup (60 mL) of butter in a heavy pot. Sauté the onions, garlic and mushrooms until the onions are translucent. Add the flour and cook for 1-2 minutes.
2. Add the wine, consommé and seasonings. Simmer to blend the flavors. Remove from the heat; keep warm while you cook the veal cutlets**.
3. The secret here is butter. Melt ¼ cup (60 mL) of butter or more in a heavy frying pan over a fairly high heat. Brown the cutlets quickly on both sides. Do not overcook.
4. Place the cutlets on a serving platter or on individual plates, if you prefer, and cover with the sauce.

Serves 6.

SERVING SUGGESTION: This is super served with Peppers and Pasta Alfredo, page 137, Caesar Salad, page 117 or 118, Aphrodisiac Green Beans, page 133, and Strawberry Temptation Puffs, page 193, for dessert.

*COOKING TIPS: ** Just a couple of hints. You can make the sauce ahead and just warm gently before serving. Also, if you cannot buy good-quality breaded cutlets, just dip the cutlets in a mixture of 1 beaten egg and ½ cup (125 mL) of milk and then into fine bread crumbs.*

* *Dymond Lake Seasoning*

Roast Lamb with Mint Jelly or Sauce

(HELEN) *If you are like the people at our house, twenty years ago you wouldn't have considered cooking lamb. Now it is a real favorite. We grow our own mint at North Knife Lake to add to our marinade and make our own mint jelly. It is the marinade that seems to give this roast such a great flavor.*

Garlic Mint Marinade:

¼ cup	salad oil	60 mL
2	garlic cloves, crushed	2
1 tbsp.	lemon juice	15 mL
2 tbsp.	crushed mint leaves	30 mL
1 tsp.	dried basil	5 mL
¼ tsp.	dried rosemary	1 mL
5 lb.	leg OR shoulder of lamb	2.5 kg

1. Combine the oil, garlic, lemon juice, mint leaves, basil and rosemary. Pour over the roast in a large shallow bowl or baking pan. Cover and marinate at least 6 hours or overnight, turning occasionally. If we are doing the 6-hour marinade, we just leave the lamb in a cool spot to come to room temperature. If we are leaving it overnight, we refrigerate it and then take it out of the refrigerator a couple of hours before cooking.
2. Place the lamb in a shallow roaster and roast at 325°F (160°C), allowing 30 minutes per pound. Baste with the marinade a couple of times during the last hour of cooking. If you are using a meat thermometer, for slightly pink lamb cook to 160-165°F (71-74°C), 170-175°F (77-80°C) for medium to well done.

Serves 8.

SERVING SUGGESTION: Greek Salad, page 114, and Len's Herbed and Spiced Oven-Roasted Potatoes, page 128, are great accompaniments for the roast lamb. Finish it off with Pavlova Nests from "Up Over", page 189.

Sheep Hunting, Anyone?

(Helen) As we have mentioned before, eating wild game is a way of life for many of us who live in the North. The difference in attitude really came home to me when my granddaughter, Rebecca, was over for dinner. She is only three but she already understands where most of the meat in the freezer comes from. Anyway, I was serving lamb for dinner and they don't eat lamb at home. She climbed up to the table, took a bite of her lamb, turned to me and said, "This is good. What is it?" I said, "It's lamb, Rebecca." "Oh" she said, "Who shot it?"

Roast Pork with
Black Currant Sauce

The black currant sauce takes this pork roast out of the everyday class and makes it downright gourmet. Marie and I especially enjoy serving this dish because we even pick the black currants and make our own jam for this one. But, if you are not fortunate enough to have a black currant patch in your back yard, just run out to your nearest supermarket and pick up a jar of jam!

4-6 lb.	boneless pork roast (we have used either a shoulder OR a loin with equally good results)	2-3 kg
2	garlic cloves, crushed	2
	DLS* OR seasoned salt and pepper	

1. While preheating the oven to 350°F (180°C), place the roast in a roaster, rub the crushed garlic cloves over the surface of the pork and then sprinkle liberally with the DLS* or seasoned salt and pepper.
2. Cook the roast until your meat thermometer reaches 170°F (77°C). Cooking time is 30 minutes per pound (500 mL).
3. While the roast is cooking, prepare the Black Currant Sauce, below.

Serves 6 but you will have sauce left over. If you are having a larger crowd just cook an 8-10 lb. (4-5 kg) roast.

SERVING SUGGESTION: This looks very attractive if you put a small glass bowl of sauce in the middle of a glass platter and surround it with the sliced pork.

* *Dymond Lake Seasoning*

Black Currant Sauce

1½ cups	black currant jam	375 mL
2 tbsp.	corn syrup	30 mL
¼ cup	red wine vinegar	60 mL
¼ tsp.	salt	1 mL
½ tsp.	cinnamon	2 mL
½ tsp.	nutmeg	2 mL
½ tsp.	cloves	2 mL
½ cup	slivered almonds	125 mL

1. Combine all the sauce ingredients except the almonds in a heavy saucepan over medium heat. Heat to boiling, reduce the heat and simmer for 2 minutes. Remove from the heat and add the almonds. Keep the sauce warm until serving time.
2. The sauce may be made ahead — just reheat over low heat before serving. It also keeps well in the refrigerator so just save any leftovers for the next time you serve roast pork.

See photograph on page 155.

Golden Glazed Ham

This is one of the most delicious recipes we have found for cooking a ham. It always turns out moist, tender and scrumptious. It's a great dish to impress the boss or to serve for an outdoor buffet.

10-15 lb.	precooked ham with OR without bone	5-7 kg
2 cups	brown sugar	500 mL
2 x 12 oz.	cans of beer (your choice)	2 x 355 mL
¼ cup	honey	60 mL
2 cups	brown sugar	500 mL
¼ cup	bourbon, rye or brandy	60 mL

1. Place the ham in a deep roasting pan. Firmly pat 2 cups (500 mL) of brown sugar over the top and sides of the ham. Pour the beer around the ham, cover and bake at 325°F (160°C) for 2½-3¾ hours (15 minutes per pound).
2. One hour before the end of the baking time, in a small saucepan, combine the honey, brown sugar and bourbon. Heat until the sugar melts.
3. Cook, uncovered, for the last hour and baste the ham every 10 minutes, first with the beer mixture from the bottom of the pan and then with the honey glaze. Use up all the glaze before removing the ham from the oven.

Serves 12-15.

SERVING SUGGESTION: Slice the ham thinly and serve it with the sauce remaining in the pan. We often team it with Parmesan Potatoes, page 129, Dilled Carrots, page 134, and Broccoli Salad, page 115. But now you try it and be the judge!

SERVING TIP: If there is a lot of fat floating on the sauce in the pan, use a baster to draw up the pure sauce from under the fat.

Clean of hands and clean of face,
I sit me down to say my grace,
God bless the food that here we see,
God bless you and God bless me.
                    Mrs. Phyllis Cormack

Hot 'N' Spicy Spareribs

This recipe has a great little "bite" to it. We team it up with Pepper and Sugar Pea Salad, page 119, and Glazed Carrots, page 134, Oven-Fried Rice, page 127, a dessert from our selection and it is a meal fit for royalty.

4 lbs.	lean pork ribs	2 kg
¾ cup	brown sugar	175 mL
¼ cup	ketchup	60 mL
¼ cup	picante* sauce	60 mL
½ cup	white vinegar	125 mL
2 tbsp.	Worcestershire sauce	30 mL
1 tsp.	chili powder	5 mL
1 cup	chopped onion	250 mL

1. Cut the ribs into approximately 3-rib pieces. Spread in the bottom of a large roaster and pour in water to a depth of about 1" (2.5 cm). Place over a burner, bring to a boil, turn down to simmer. Cover and simmer for 1½ hours. Remove from the heat and pour off the water (or save and degrease for soup stock).
2. Mix all of the remaining ingredients together in a mixing bowl or large measuring cup and pour over the drained ribs.
3. Bake, UNCOVERED, at 250°F (130°C) for 2 hours, stirring occasionally.

Serves 6 .

* *Picante means HOT in Spanish. There are several brands of hot pepper sauce available. Use one that creates the amount of fire you want.*

For each new morning with its Light,
For rest and shelter of the night,
For health and food, for love and friends,
For everything Thy goodness sends,
We thank Thee, Lord.
Ralph Waldo Emerson (1803 — 1882)

Len's Delicious Honey-Ginger Ribs

Here's that Len again! These ribs are some of the finest we have ever tasted. This recipe is definitely best with nice tender baby back ribs.

	ribs to feed the size of the crowd you are feeding. We find that ¾ lb. (365 g) per person is a good rule of thumb.	
¼ cup	peeled, sliced fresh ginger	60 mL
2 tbsp.	ketchup	30 mL
2 tbsp.	soy sauce	30 mL
2	garlic cloves, crushed	2
	Thick and Spicy Honey-Flavored Barbecue Sauce by Kraft OR the equivalent.	

1. Cut the ribs into about 3" (7 cm) pieces.
2. Put about ½" (1.3 cm) of water in the bottom of a roasting pan and add the ginger, ketchup, soy sauce and garlic.
3. If you have a steamer, place that in the water and pile the ribs on top. I have had good success with just placing the ribs in the water. Just be sure there is not too much water, and do keep an eye on it. Add more water during cooking, if necessary.
4. Cover the ribs and steam for 1½ hours on top of the stove.
5. Remove the ribs from the pan.
6. At this point you should have your barbecue hot. Place the ribs on the barbecue, brush with the barbecue sauce and cook for about 3 minutes. Turn, brush with more sauce and cook another 3-5 minutes until nicely glazed.
7. EAT!!!!!!

NOTE: We have also done the steaming ahead so that the ribs were cold when they went on the grill. Just increase the cooking time about 5 minutes to be sure they are piping hot.

How long a fish grows depends on how long you listen to the fisherman.

Sweet 'N' Sour Beans and Ribs

This is a great dish to serve if you want to spend the afternoon on an outing with family and friends and then bring them home for a special dinner. Just add a big bowl of coleslaw, pull some crusty rolls out of the freezer and you are all set!

2 cups	dried white beans	500 mL
6 cups	cold water	1.5 L
3 lbs.	spareribs	1.5 kg
	garlic powder and salt to taste	
1 cup	chopped onion	250 mL
¼ cup	cider vinegar	60 mL
⅛ tsp.	allspice	0.5 mL
1½ tsp.	dry mustard	7 mL
2 tsp.	salt	10 mL
¼ tsp.	pepper	1 mL
⅓ cup	brown sugar	75 mL
2 tbsp.	molasses	30 mL
½ tsp.	ground ginger	2 mL
2	garlic cloves, crushed	2
5½ oz.	can tomato paste	156 mL

1. Place the beans and cold water in a large pot. Soak the beans overnight. The next day put the pot on the stove, bring to a boil and then simmer until the beans are tender, 1-2 hours. Drain the beans and reserve 2 cups (500 mL) of the liquid.
2. Cut the ribs into serving-sized pieces, about 3 ribs each. Place the ribs on a broiler pan or baking sheet. Broil 5-10 minutes to brown.
3. Mix cooked beans, reserved liquid, onion, vinegar, allspice, mustard, salt, pepper, brown sugar, molasses, ginger, garlic and tomato paste in a large roaster.
4. Place the ribs on top of the beans and bake at 250°F (120°C) for 3½ hours. Increase the oven temperature to 350°F (180°C), remove the cover and cook for another 30 minutes.

Serves 4-6.

Honey Garlic Cornish Game Hens

(HELEN) This elegant dish always impresses the guests. I almost hate to put it in here because they are going to find out just how easy it is.

4	Cornish game hens	4
	DLS* OR salt and pepper	
	vegetable oil	
1 tbsp.	freshly grated ginger OR 1½ tsp. (7 mL) dried	15 mL
2	garlic cloves, crushed	2
¼ cup	melted butter OR margarine	60 mL
¾ cup	soy sauce	175 mL
¼ cup	honey	60 mL

1. Place the hens on a baking sheet with sides, such as a jelly-roll pan or broiler pan. Rub a little oil on the hens, then sprinkle them with DLS* or salt and pepper. Roast in 400°F (200°C) oven for 15 minutes.
2. Combine ginger, garlic, butter, soy sauce and honey in a saucepan. Heat and stir until blended and hot.
3. Remove the hens from the oven and baste with about ⅓ of the sauce. Return to the oven and lower the temperature to 350°F (180°C). Continue roasting until done, approximately 1 hour, basting every 15 minutes with the remainder of the sauce.

Serves 6.

SERVING SUGGESTION: To serve, cut game hens in halves or quarters. These look very nice laid on a platter, breast side up, garnished with parsley or fresh mint leaves. We usually team them up with Marie's Wild Rice Casserole Suprême, page 126, buttered broccoli and our Mushroom Bacon Spinach Salad, page 116. We invite you to let your imagination go and come up with your own combination!

* *Dymond Lake Seasoning*

The perils of duck hunting are great — especially for the duck!

Sour Cream Chicken or Pork Chops

(HELEN) This is another recipe that came to us via brother-in-law Len, a number of years ago. The subtle flavor of dill makes this an appealing entrée.

10-12	pieces of chicken OR pork chops	10-12
	butter OR margarine	
	DLS* OR salt, pepper and paprika	
2 x 10 oz.	cans mushroom soup	2 x 284 mL
1½ oz.	pkg. onion soup mix	40 g
1 tbsp.	lemon juice	15 mL
1 tsp.	dillweed	5 mL
1 cup	sour cream	250 mL

1. Melt ¼ cup (60 mL) or less butter in a frying pan**. Add chicken pieces and sprinkle with DLS* or salt, pepper and paprika. Cook until chicken is browned nicely and remove the meat to a casserole or roaster.
2. Combine mushroom soup, onion soup mix, lemon juice, dillweed and sour cream. Pour over the chicken in the casserole or roaster.
3. Cover and bake at 350°F (180°C) for 1½ hours. We usually stir it once during baking.

Serves 8.

SERVING SUGGESTION: *Serve with medium egg noodles, a green salad, buttered carrots, fresh rolls and any of our desserts for a grand finish.*

NOTE: *This recipe really does take the full hour and a half to cook. It also doubles and triples very well but you do have to allow a little extra cooking time (10-15 minutes).*

* *Dymond Lake Seasoning*
** *ALTERNATE BROWNING METHOD: Place the chicken on a greased baking sheet. Brush with melted butter. Sprinkle with seasonings. Roast in a 425°F (220°C) oven for 30 minutes, or until well browned.*

Pork

Roast Pork with Black Currant Sauce, page 148
Aphrodisiac Green Beans, page 133
Len's Herbed and Spiced Oven-Roasted Potatoes, page 128
French Bread, page 44

Tame Meats

Chicken Cacciatore

This is a simple yet elegant taste treat, for busy cooks. Team it up with spaghetti or your favorite pasta and sit back and watch it disappear.

16	pieces frying chicken	16
½ cup	flour	125 mL
1 tsp.	salt	5 mL
¼ cup	butter OR margarine	60 mL
¼ cup	olive oil	60 mL
2	medium onions, sliced	2
1	green pepper, sliced	1
1 lb.	fresh mushrooms, sliced	500 g
2	garlic cloves, crushed	2
28 oz.	can tomatoes, drained and chopped, reserve the juice	796 mL
2	chicken bouillon cubes (2 tsp. [10 mL])	2
2 tbsp.	chopped fresh parsley OR 2 tsp. (10 mL) dried	30 mL
1½ tsp.	salt	7 mL
¼ tsp.	pepper	1 mL
½ tsp.	dried oregano	2 mL
½ tsp.	dried marjoram	2 mL
½ tsp.	dried thyme	2 mL
½ cup	dry white wine*	125 mL
½ cup	sliced ripe Italian olives	125 mL
	Parmesan cheese	

1. Dredge chicken pieces in flour and salt. Brown in a mixture of butter and olive oil in a large frying pan. Remove to a 5-quart (5 L) casserole.
2. In the same frying pan, sauté the onion, green pepper, mushrooms and garlic until tender-crisp. Stir in the tomatoes, bouillon cubes, parsley, seasonings, white wine and ½ cup (125 mL) of the reserved tomato juice. Cook a few minutes to blend and add to the chicken in the casserole, cover and bake at 350°F (180°C) for 45 minutes. Remove the cover, add the olives and bake for another 15-20 minutes.
3. Remove the chicken and vegetables to a platter and keep them warm.
4. Rapidly boil the liquid in the pan until it is slightly reduced and thickened. Pour over the chicken and sprinkle with Parmesan cheese.

Serves 10-12.

* *Use water or more of the reserved tomato juice instead of white wine.*

Polar Bear and Cub –

A common sight in Churchill, Manitoba, the Polar Bear Capitol of the World! (Photo by Mike Macri.)

Saucy Sweet 'N' Sour Chicken Legs

This is a saucy little chicken dish. It is easy and delicious and makes lots of sauce, so it is great with rice.

12	chicken pieces (we count the thigh and leg as 2 pieces)	12
½ cup	flour	125 mL
2 tsp.	DLS* OR 1 tsp. (5 mL) salt and ½ tsp. (2 mL) pepper	10 mL
1 cup	brown sugar	250 mL
1 cup	white vinegar	250 mL
1 cup	white wine**	250 mL
¼ cup	soy sauce	60 mL

1. Shake the chicken pieces in the flour mixed with seasonings. You may brown them either in a heavy skillet with a little oil, or use our preferred method — on a greased (sprayed) cookie sheet in the oven. Place a single layer on the cookie sheet and bake them at 425°F (220°C) for 30 minutes, turning once. Transfer the pieces to a 3-quart (3 L) roaster or casserole.
2. Mix together the sugar, vinegar, white wine and soy sauce and pour over the chicken.
3. Reduce the oven temperature to 350°F (180°C) and continue to cook the chicken, uncovered, for 40-50 minutes, turning once.

Serves 6.

* *Dymond Lake Seasoning*
** *For everyday use, water is a good substitute.*

Fishin'

"How are the fish in these parts?" said I.
The red-faced angler looked up with a sigh.
"Well," said he, "I really can't say.
For a week I've dropped them a line each day,
But so far I've had no reply."

Tame Meats

Liz's Peach-Glazed Chicken

(HELEN) This recipe came from one of our competitors who owns the SECOND best lodge in Manitoba! That is just a little internal competition that we have going. Actually she and her husband, Ike, are very dear friends. Liz and I swap recipes frequently. We know she'll get a kick out of seeing this in OUR book.

2	fryer chickens cut up OR equivalent pieces	2
½ cup	flour	125 mL
2 tsp.	DLS* OR ½ tsp. (2 mL) EACH salt and pepper and 1 tsp. (5 mL) seasoned salt	10 mL
1	large onion, thinly sliced	1
1½ cups	peach jam	375 mL
1½ cups	regular barbecue sauce	375 mL
3 tbsp.	soy sauce	45 mL
1	green pepper, thinly sliced	1

1. Shake the chicken in a mixture of the flour and seasonings.
2. Brown the chicken either in a frying pan or on greased cookie pans in a 425°F (220°C) oven for 30 minutes, turning once. Remove to a 4-quart (4 L) roaster or casserole. Spread the sliced onions over the chicken.
3. Mix together the peach jam, barbecue sauce and soy sauce. Pour over the chicken and cover.
4. Bake in a 350°F (180°C) oven for 45 minutes. Remove the cover and add the green pepper. Continue to cook, uncovered, for 10-15 minutes.

Serves 8.

* *Dymond Lake Seasoning*

Two old cronies were fishing together at about the same place in the stream. One man had been having excellent luck, landing some real beauties. But the other man was doing no good at all.

"What's the matter?" asked the lucky fisherman, "Why do you suppose you haven't caught any? We're both at the same place in the stream and, by George, we're even using the same kind of bait."

"Search me," answered the second man. "Maybe my worm isn't trying!"

Crispy Oven-Fried Chicken

For those of you who love fried chicken as much as we do but also hate the clean up and extra calories of the deep- or pan-frying. This recipe is exceptional when you use the DLS* in it but we have also given you a good substitute.

1 cup	very finely crushed saltine crackers	250 mL
¼ cup	grated Parmesan cheese	60 mL
1 tbsp.	DLS* OR substitute below	15 mL
½ tsp.	salt	2 mL
6 lbs.	chicken pieces (2 fryers, cut up)	3 kg
½ cup	evaporated milk	125 mL
⅓ cup	cooking oil	75 mL

1. Combine the crackers, cheese, DLS* and salt in a bowl or heavy plastic bag.
2. Dip the chicken pieces in the evaporated milk and then shake or roll them in the crumb mixture.
3. Place the pieces on a greased baking tray, skin side up. Bake at 375°F (190°C) for 30 minutes. Brush with oil and continue to bake for another 30 minutes.

Serves 8.

* *Dymond Lake Seasoning substitute for this recipe:*

½ tsp.	oregano	2 mL
½ tsp.	basil	2 mL
½ tsp.	celery salt	2 mL
½ tsp.	onion salt	2 mL
¼ tsp.	paprika	1 mL
¼ tsp.	pepper	1 mL
¼ tsp.	garlic powder	1 mL

Lord, bless our ears with Your word,
Bless our bodies with Your bounties,
Bless our lives with Your love.
Mount St. Mary's Abbey, Massachusetts

 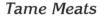 *Tame Meats*

Roast Turkey with Stuffing & Gravy

(HELEN) When Jeannie, our second daughter, was 14 (she is now married and has two daughters of her own), she ended up out at North Knife Lake cooking for a group of fishermen. At that time, the only contact we had was by radio. One morning at our scheduled radio time, this little voice over the airwaves said "Mom, how do you cook a turkey?" Here she was, about to cook her first turkey and feed it to paying guests! and, she couldn't find a recipe even though there were plenty of cookbooks at the lake. So, this recipe is for all of you aspiring young cooks!

Don't be intimidated by the length of this recipe — remember it is really three recipes — Roast Turkey, Stuffing and Gravy. We wanted to give enough instructions so that, even if it is your first turkey dinner, you won't be disappointed.

Roast Turkey with Stuffing

1 cup	chopped onion	250 mL
1/2 cup	chopped celery	125 mL
1/2 cup	butter OR margarine	125 mL
8 cups	cubed soft bread* (white, brown OR mixed)	2 L
2 tsp.	poultry seasoning	10 mL
1/2 tsp.	sage	2 mL
1 tsp.	salt	5 mL
1/4 tsp.	pepper	1 mL
1/2 cup	water (approximately)	125 mL
12-14 lb.	turkey, thawed	6-7 kg
1/4 cup	butter OR margarine, melted	60 mL
	DLS** OR seasoned salt and pepper	
	giblets (neck, liver, heart that you found inside the turkey)	

1. Sauté the onions and celery in 1/2 cup (125 mL) butter until soft.
2. Put the cubed bread into a large bowl. Add the cooked onion and celery mixture and the seasonings. Add enough water to make the mixture moist but not soggy, about 1/2 cup (125 mL).
3. Rinse out the cavity of the thawed turkey; shake out any excess water. Stuff the dressing into the turkey cavity and into the space at the neck. I slip the ends of the legs back into the band of skin at the base of the cavity opening to keep the body stuffing in place and just pull the neck skin down and tuck it under to keep the neck stuffing in place. If all the stuffing doesn't fit, put the extra in a small casserole, pour 1/2 cup (125 mL) of the broth from the neck and giblets (see step 6) over it and put it in the oven with the turkey for the last 1 1/2 hours.

Roast Turkey with Stuffing

Continued

4. Place the turkey in a roaster. Brush melted butter on the skin of the turkey and sprinkle very liberally with spices — DLS* if you have it, seasoned salt and pepper if you don't.

5. Put the turkey, UNCOVERED, into a preheated 325°F (160°C) oven. Allow 5 hours for cooking, approximately 25 minutes per pound (500 g). If after 4 hours or so it seems to be getting too brown you can cover it either with the lid or loosely with foil. Remember, though, that a nice dark brown turkey makes for great gravy. When it is done you should be able to pull a leg off without difficulty and the juices that run out should not be pink. (But do not cook so much that no juices run out.) If you are using a thermometer it should register 190°F (95°C) when it is inserted in the thigh. Be sure not to let it touch the bone.)

6. While the turkey is cooking, take the neck and the giblets from the cavity, put them in a saucepan and cover them with 8 cups (2 L) of water. Bring to a boil and simmer for a couple of hours, adding more water if necessary. Use this to pour over the extra stuffing, in the gravy or in the turkey soup you are going to make with all your leftovers (see Turkey Carcass Soup, page 74).

7. When the turkey is done remove it from the roaster to a baking pan with sides, as it will be dripping some juice. Now get somebody to carve it while you make the gravy. Or else you carve it and get somebody else to make the gravy. Or tent it lightly with foil and let it rest for 15-20 minutes while you make the gravy.

* We use leftover bread that we have been saving daily. It is a good idea to keep a bag in the freezer to collect those crusts and almost stale bread that you might normally throw away.

** Dymond Lake Seasoning

Thank you for the world so sweet,
Thank you for the food we eat.
Thank you for the birds that sing,
Thank you, Lord, for everything.
                    E. Rutter Leatham

 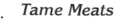

Turkey Gravy

I am going to give you two methods for making gravy and let you take your pick. If you are inexperienced, I would suggest you opt for measuring the drippings.

Method 1:

1. POUR THE DRIPPINGS OUT OF THE PAN leaving behind all the nice brown bits.
2. Measure the drippings and return 1 cup (250 mL) of drippings to the pan. Put some heat under the roaster and heat until the drippings are bubbly, then REMOVE FROM HEAT.
3. Using a wire whisk, whisk 1 cup (250 mL) of flour into the drippings, being sure to scrape the browned bits off the bottom of the pan. Whisk until smooth. At this point you can start adding very hot water, 1 CUP (250 mL) AT A TIME to begin with, whisking until smooth. (I use the water I have boiled my potatoes in and the water from the neck and giblets.) Add the rest of the water more quickly, but stop at 7 cups (1.75 L).
4. PUT THE ROASTER BACK ON THE HEAT. Bring to a boil, stirring constantly. Turn the heat down and simmer for a few minutes. At this point add a little more water if it is too thick and add 1 tsp. (5 mL) of salt and ½ tsp. (2 mL) of pepper. Taste and add more seasoning if it needs it. Keep warm over very low heat until you are ready to serve.

Method 2:

1. REMOVE THE PAN FROM THE HEAT. TO THE HOT DRIPPINGS IN THE PAN, add flour, whisking constantly until all the drippings are absorbed. Slowly start adding your liquid, still whisking constantly.
2. When you have your first 7 cups (1.75 L) of liquid in, put the roaster on the heat and bring to a boil, stirring constantly. Add salt and pepper to taste. Add more liquid if necessary and keep warm until ready to serve.
3. This method of adding the flour to the hot drippings rather than mixing the flour and water makes a much superior gravy. It is a little trickier but as long as you get the fat hot, remove the roaster from the heat and don't put it back on the heat until after you have added the liquid, you should have no trouble

Trapper Don
"Bear Guide of the North"

(HELEN) *It was another warm day in July and once again we were at Dymond Lake. This time we were involved in a Guide Training Course for young people interested in working in the hunting and fishing industry in Northern Manitoba. Trapper Don was in charge of the fishing and hunting segments of the course and Bonnie, our local naturalist, was in charge of the natural history, flora and fauna segments.*

To really appreciate this story, you have to have some background on Trapper Don. At this stage of his life, his main claim to fame was that he was the No. 1 black bear guide in Manitoba and he looked the part. He is a big burly man with a nice thick, bushy beard and looks just like your idea of Mr. Bushman. But, he had never seen a POLAR BEAR and he really wanted to see one. Well, one morning, Bonnie had the group out teaching them all about the birds and the bees and the flowers and the trees and anything else they could find. Don was relaxing in the lounge and I was (where else?) in the kitchen making lunch. I happened to look out the window and what to my wondering eyes did appear but a nice fluffy white polar bear heading straight for the lodge. I called to Don to come and see the bear he had been wanting to see, expecting nothing but calm delight from this experienced bushman. Well, you should have seen the excitement! He came running over to have a look and then immediately got into a bit of a panic about what we should do. I assured him that I was going to continue to make lunch and just keep an eye on where the bear went. That just would not do for Don, he thought we should get on the roof until Bonnie came back since she had the only firearm in camp with her. I thought that might not be such a bad idea as it was a lovely warm day and we would be able to get a good view of the bear from the roof and besides, I thought it might calm Don down a bit. There was already a ladder leading up to the roof so out we went. Well, the next thing I knew, I was standing on the ground looking up at Don who had almost flown up to the roof. My first question was "Whatever happened to women and children first, Don?" His very embarrassed reply was "Please don't tell my wife about this."

Mr. Bear did what I thought he would and just kept wandering north but Don's actions have given me a lot of ammunition for teasing him when we meet up at the sport shows or outfitters' conventions!

Tame Meats

Final Temptations

When you think your tummy has taken all it can hold we are bound to arrive with a dessert so tempting it elicits groans from many guests. The mind says no but the "flesh is weak". A refusal is rare. Usually an assurance from one of us that we remove all the calories in the kitchen is enough to win them over. (Just a little white lie.)

Peach or Nectarine Roll

This roll, and its cousin, the chocolate roll, can be made early on the same day you are serving it or it can be made well in advance. It needs some time in the freezer. Pull THIS out of your freezer for unexpected company, they'll be impressed.

Cake:

4	eggs	4
¾ cup	sugar	175 mL
1 tsp.	vanilla	5 mL
¾ cup	flour (minus 1 tbsp.)	160 mL
¾ tsp.	baking powder	3 mL
¼ tsp.	salt	1 mL
	icing sugar	

Peach or Nectarine Filling:

1 cup	whipping cream	250 mL
3 tbsp.	sugar	45 mL
¼ tsp.	vanilla	1 mL
¾ cup	diced fresh peaches OR nectarines	175 mL

1. To make the cake, prepare a 1 x 10½ x 15½" (2.5 x 26.3 x 39.3 cm) jelly roll pan by greasing it and lining it with waxed paper. Have the paper extend over the ends of the pan.
2. Beat eggs, sugar and vanilla in a large mixing bowl with an electric mixer at high speed until light and lemon-colored.
3. Sift together flour, baking powder and salt.
4. Add to the egg mixture, mixing lightly with a spoon or spatula.
5. Spread batter in a waxed paper-lined pan.
6. Bake in a 375°F (190°C) oven for 15 minutes, or until cake springs back when touched.
7. While the cake is baking, lay out a clean tea towel on a flat surface and sift icing sugar over it, to lightly cover the towel.
8. Loosen the cake from the sides of the pan. Invert onto the tea towel.
9. Immediately remove the waxed paper from the cake by pulling gently and steadily from one end. Trim off any dry edges.
10. Roll up the cake with the towel, starting the roll at a 10½" (26.3 cm) side. Place it on a cooling rack and allow it to cool completely.
11. To prepare the filling, whip the cream until it begins to thicken. Gradually add sugar, beating until thick. Add vanilla. Fold in peaches.
12. To assemble the roll, unroll the cooled cake carefully.
13. Spread the filling evenly over the cake.
14. Roll the cake back up again and wrap it in the tea towel.
15. Place the cake in the freezer until 15 minutes before serving time.
   18. If you are not serving the roll until another day, put it in something airtight for storage in the freezer.

Desserts

Peach or Nectarine Roll

Continued

Peach Topping:

2 cups	diced fresh peaches	500 mL
1/3 cup	sugar	75 mL
3/4 cup	water	175 mL
2 tbsp.	cornstarch	30 mL
1/4 cup	cold water	60 mL

19. To prepare the topping, put the peaches, sugar and 3/4 cup (175 mL) water in a saucepan. Bring to a boil. Simmer for 10 minutes.
20. Mix cornstarch with 1/4 cup (60 mL) water. Add to the peach mixture and continue cooking, stirring constantly, until the mixture thickens.
21. Let cool. Keep refrigerated until serving time.

Serves 10.

SERVING SUGGESTION: Slice the peach roll in 1" (2.5 cm) slices. Spoon about 1/3 cup (75 mL) peach topping over each slice. Top with whipped cream, if desired.

Chocolate Cake Roll

A close cousin to the Peach Roll, this might be called the black sheep of the jelly roll family. Same basic recipe, different taste.

Cake:
Follow the cake recipe for Peach Roll but add 1/4 cup (60 mL) cocoa with the flour.

Filling:
Follow the filling recipe for Peach Roll omitting the peaches.

Chocolate Topping:

2 x 1 oz.	squares unsweetened chocolate	2 x 30 g
1/4 cup	butter OR margarine	60 mL
1 1/8 cups	evaporated milk	280 mL
1 1/2 cups	sugar	375 mL

1. To prepare the topping, combine the chocolate, butter and milk in a saucepan and heat over medium heat, stirring constantly, until the butter and chocolate are melted.
2. Slowly add sugar and cook until the sugar dissolves.
3. Remove from the heat, let cool, and refrigerate until ready to serve.
4. To put it all together, follow the recipe for Peach Roll, but sift icing sugar over the chocolate roll before freezing.

Serves 10.

SERVING SUGGESTIONS: Serve with whipped cream or ice cream.

Cranberry Cake with Butter Sauce

This dessert is a real sleeper. To read it, it sounds "ho hum" but the first bite will pop your eyes wide open. This recipe keeps Marie and me crawling around on the tundra, making sure we have our winter supply of cranberries in the freezer.

3 cups	flour	750 mL
4 tsp.	baking powder	20 mL
½ tsp.	salt	2 mL
3 tbsp.	butter OR margarine	45 mL
1½ cups	sugar	375 mL
1½ tsp.	vanilla	7 mL
1½ cups	milk	375 mL
3 cups	cranberries	750 mL

1. Mix the flour, baking powder and salt in a bowl and set aside.
2. Cream together the butter, sugar and vanilla. It does not get all creamy and fluffy as it does in a butter cake, as the ratio of butter to sugar is not high enough. That is the way it is supposed to be.
3. Add the flour mixture to the creamed mixture alternately with the milk, beating after each addition, just until it is mixed.
4. Stir in the cranberries. (If you are using large commercial cranberries, chop them up a bit. Try a quick whir in the food processor.)
5. Spread the batter in a greased 9 x 13" (23 x 33 cm) pan. Bake in a 400°F (200°C) oven for 30-40 minutes, until golden brown and the top springs back when lightly touched.

Butter Sauce

¾ cup	butter OR margarine	175 mL
1½ cups	sugar	375 mL
¾ cup	evaporated milk OR cream	175 mL

1. Combine the sauce ingredients in a saucepan and bring to a boil over medium heat, stirring constantly. Simmer for 2 minutes and remove from heat. A wire whisk is very useful to keep the sauce smooth.

Makes a 9 x 13" (23 x 33 cm) cake.

SERVING SUGGESTION: Serve the sauce warm over the cake — and remember — the secret is in the sauce. Be prepared for raves! (ummm! ahhh! ohhh!)

NOTE: If you want to make this in a 9" (23 cm) square pan, just cut back on the ingredients by ⅓.

See photograph on page 173.

Helen's Heavenly Cake

A basic chocolate cake recipe that lends itself to these two variations, among others. If you want to use it as a birthday cake, use Jeanne's Bakery Icing. It sets well, can be easily decorated and isn't too sweet. For a more elegant dessert, use the Orange Cream Filling. A wonderful blend of flavors that will temptingly tease your taste buds.

¾ cup	butter OR margarine	175 mL
2 cups	sugar	500 mL
2	eggs	2
1 tsp.	vanilla	5 mL
2½ cups	flour	625 mL
½ cup	cocoa	125 mL
2 tsp.	baking soda	10 mL
½ tsp.	salt	2 mL
2 cups	buttermilk OR sour milk*	500 mL

1. To prepare the cake, in a large mixing bowl, cream together butter and sugar. Add eggs and vanilla and mix well.
2. In another bowl, mix flour, cocoa, baking soda and salt.
3. Add flour mixture to creamed mixture alternately with buttermilk, making 3 dry and 2 liquid additions, starting and ending with the flour. Mix just until blended.
4. Spread batter in well-greased baking pans, either a 9 x 13" (23 x 33 cm) pan or 2, 8" (20 cm) round pans**.
5. Bake in a 350°F (180°C) oven for 40 minutes, or until a toothpick inserted in the center comes out dry. Let the cake cool in the pan for 5 minutes before turning out on a rack to cool.

* *For sour milk, add 2 tbsp. (30 mL) lemon juice or vinegar to 1⅞ cups (460 mL) milk.*
** *If making the Orange Cream Filling, use 2, 8" (20 cm) round pans.*

Jeanne's Quick Icing

3¾ oz	pkg. instant chocolate pudding	113 g
1 cup	whipping cream	250 mL

1. Prepare the pudding according to the package directions.
2. Whip the cream until stiff.
3. Fold the whipped cream into the pudding mix and spread over the cooled cake.

Jeanne's Bakery Icing

There is a Jeanne's Bakery in Winnipeg, Manitoba, and family history has it that my aunt got this recipe there. It has been used for decorating birthday cakes in our family for over 30 years. It is a nice soft icing and it holds its shape. It can be used for making designs on a cake and if you mess up you just smooth it over or scoop it off and start again. It also takes food coloring very well.

¼ cup	flour	60 mL
1 cup	milk	250 mL
1 cup	shortening	250 mL
1 cup	icing sugar	250 mL
¼ tsp.	salt	1 mL
1 tsp.	vanilla	10 mL

1. Blend the flour with ¼ cup (60 mL) milk in a small saucepan. Gradually add the remaining milk, stirring to avoid lumps. It helps to use a whisk. If, at this point, you DO have some lumps (nobody's perfect) strain them out of your mixture. Cook and stir constantly, over medium heat, until thick. Set aside to cool.
2. In a medium-sized bowl, cream together shortening, sugar, salt and vanilla.
3. Add the flour mixture, 1 tbsp. (15 mL) at a time, to the sugar mixture, beating constantly.
4. Spread over the cake.

VARIATIONS: For Chocolate Icing, melt 1 cup (250 mL) chocolate chips, let cool slightly and add after step #3. To use some of the icing for decorating, set aside ½ cup (125 mL) white icing, add food coloring, and get creative!

Orange Cream Filling

¾ cup	frozen concentrated orange juice	175 mL
¾ cup	sugar	175 mL
1 tbsp.	gelatin (1 envelope)	15 mL
2	oranges, coarsely grated peel of	2
¼ cup	Cointreau OR Grand Marnier (optional)	60 mL
2 cups	whipping cream	500 mL
¾ cup	icing sugar	175 mL
1 oz.	square semisweet chocolate, shaved	30 g

1. Combine orange juice, sugar and gelatin in a saucepan. Cook over medium heat, stirring constantly until sugar and gelatin are completely dissolved, about 5 minutes.

Orange Cream Filling

Continued

2. Remove from the heat and stir in orange peel and Cointreau, if using.
3. Allow the orange mixture to cool. To prevent a crust from forming on top, either stir every 5 minutes or press a piece of waxed paper to the surface and refrigerate until the filling no longer feels warm, approximately 20 minutes.
4. Meanwhile, whip the cream in a large bowl until soft peaks form. Gradually add icing sugar, beating well.
5. Fold cooled orange mixture into whipped cream.
6. Slice each 8" (20 cm) round cake in half horizontally, to make 4 layers.
7. Place 1 layer of cake, cut side up, on a serving plate. Spread ¼ of the filling over the layer. Top with another layer and continue until all are used. A layer of orange cream will be on top.
8. Top with curls of shaved, semisweet chocolate.
9. Refrigerate for a few hours before serving.

Serves 16.

Get ready to impress your guests!

Calories

Methuselah ate what he found on his plate,
And never, as people do now,
Did he note the amount of caloric count —
He ate it because it was chow.

He wasn't disturbed, as at dinner he sat,
Destroying a roast or a pie,
To think it was lacking in granular fat,
Or a couple of vitamins shy.

He cheerfully chewed every species of food,
Undisturbed by worries or fears,
Lest his health might be hurt by some fancy dessert,
And he lived over nine hundred years!

Triple Chocolate Cake

This one will send your chocoholic taste buds just a-dancing.

19 oz.	pkg. Dark Devils Food cake mix	520 g
1 cup	sour cream	250 mL
3¾ oz.	pkg. instant chocolate pudding mix	113 g
½ cup	vegetable oil	125 mL
½ cup	warm water	125 mL
4	eggs, beaten	4
1½ cups	semisweet chocolate chips	375 mL

1. In a large mixing bowl combine the first 6 ingredients. Beat for 4 minutes. Fold in the chocolate chips.
2. Pour into a greased and floured* 12-cup (3 L) bundt pan and bake at 350°F (180°C) for 50-60 minutes, or until a toothpick inserted in the center comes out clean.
3. Cool the cake in the pan on a rack for 15 minutes and then turn out onto the serving plate.

Serves 16.

SERVING SUGGESTION: *A dollop of whipped cream and a bit of shaved semisweet chocolate over the top of each piece finishes this off nicely. It is also delicious served with strawberries or kiwi fruit.*

* *We use an environmentally safe cooking spray at the lake and find that it is not really necessary to flour.*

NOTE: *See the Scratch Model Triple Chocolate Cake on page 175, if you don't have a cake mix in your cupboard.*

Wild Berry Desserts

Cranberry Cake with Butter Sauce, page 168
Pavlova Nests from "Up Over" with Wild Blueberries, page 189

Triple Chocolate Cake
(Scratch Model)

If you don't have a cake mix handy, try this version.

½ cup	butter OR margarine	125 mL
2 cups	white sugar	500 mL
4	eggs	4
½ cup	vegetable oil	125 mL
½ cup	warm water	125 mL
1 cup	sour cream	250 mL
2½ cups	flour	625 mL
½ cup	cocoa	125 mL
2 tsp.	baking soda	10 mL
½ tsp.	salt	2 mL
3¾ oz.	pkg. instant chocolate pudding	113 g
1½ cups	chocolate chips	375 mL

1. In a large bowl, with an electric mixer, cream together butter and sugar. Add eggs and beat well.
2. In a separate bowl, combine oil, water and sour cream.
3. In another bowl, combine the remaining dry ingredients.
4. Add the liquid mixture to the creamed mixture, alternately with the dry ingredients, beating well after each addition. Beat until very creamy.
5. Fold in the chocolate chips.
6. Pour into a greased and floured* 12-cup (3 L) bundt pan and bake at 350°F (180°C) for 50-60 minutes, or until a toothpick inserted in the center comes out clean.
7. Cool the cake in the pan on a rack for 15 minutes and then turn out onto the serving plate.

Serves 16.

* *We use a cooking spray at the lake and find that it is not really necessary to flour.*

Willow Ptarmigan
(Photo by Dennis Fast.)

14 Carat Cake

This is by far the best carrot cake we have ever found. We have tried a few others but we keep going back to this one! If we are cooking it for the family we usually use an oblong pan but if you cook it in a bundt pan it is fancy enough to bring out for company!

2 cups	flour	500 mL
2 tsp.	baking powder	10 mL
1½ tsp.	baking soda	7 mL
1 tsp.	salt	5 mL
2 tsp.	ground cinnamon	10 mL
2 cups	sugar	500 mL
1½ cups	salad oil	375 mL
4	eggs	4
2 cups	finely shredded carrots	500 mL
1 cup	drained, crushed pineapple	250 mL
½ cup	chopped pecans	125 mL
1 cup	finely shredded coconut (optional)	250 mL

1. Mix the flour, baking powder, baking soda, salt and cinnamon in a large mixing bowl.
2. Add the sugar, oil and eggs. Beat with an electric mixer at medium speed for 1 minute.
3. Stir in the carrots, pineapple, pecans and coconut, if using.
4. Turn into a greased, 9 x 13" (23 x 33 cm) or bundt pan and bake in a 350°F (180°C) oven for 50-60 minutes. Start checking at 50 minutes as you do not want the cake to dry out.
5. Cool the cake in the pan on a cooling rack. If you have baked the cake in a bundt pan, remove from pan after it has cooled for 10 minutes.
6. When the cake has cooled, frost with Cream Cheese Icing, below.

Serves 15.

Cream Cheese Icing

8 oz.	cream cheese at room temperature	250 g
½ cup	butter OR margarine	125 mL
1 tsp.	vanilla	5 mL
4 cups	icing sugar	1 L

1. Cream the cheese, butter and vanilla together with an electric mixer at medium speed. Gradually add the icing sugar, beating well until smooth and creamy. If the mixture is too stiff to spread, add milk, 1 tbsp. (15 mL) at a time, until it reaches spreading consistency.

Fruit Cocktail Cake

This should be called Old Faithful. It is very easy and we know of no better last minute dessert — 5 minutes and it is ready for the oven. Quick, easy and delicious!

Cake:

1½ cups	sugar	375 mL
2 cups	flour	500 mL
2 tsp.	baking soda	10 mL
½ tsp.	salt	2 mL
2	eggs	2
14 oz.	can fruit cocktail, undrained OR crushed pineapple OR peaches, chopped	398 mL

Gooey Topping:

¾ cup	sugar	175 mL
½ cup	cream OR evaporated milk	125 mL
½ cup	butter OR margarine	125 mL
1 tsp.	vanilla	5 mL

1. In a large bowl, mix together all of the cake ingredients, including the fruit liquid. Pour into a greased 9 x 13" (23 x 33 cm) pan.
2. Bake at 350°F (180°C) for 30-40 minutes, or until the top springs back when touched lightly in the middle.
3. While the cake is baking, prepare the topping. In a small saucepan, bring the sugar, cream and butter to a boil. Simmer for about 1 minute, remove from the heat and add the vanilla.
4. Pour the hot topping over the cake when you remove it from the oven. The sauce soaks into the cake, making a simple cake taste delectable.

Serves 12-15.

Lemon Pudding Cake

This is an absolutely luscious lemon dessert. Light, airy and very lemony.

4	eggs, separated	4
1/3 cup	lemon juice*	75 mL
1 tsp.	dried grated lemon rind OR 2 tsp. (10 mL) freshly grated lemon rind	5 mL
1 tbsp.	melted butter OR margarine	15 mL
1 1/2 cups	sugar	375 mL
1/2 cup	flour	125 mL
1/2 tsp.	salt	2 mL
1 1/2 cups	milk	375 mL

1. Beat together the egg yolks, lemon juice, lemon rind and melted butter with an electric beater until thick and a light lemon colour, about 5 minutes.
2. In a separate bowl combine sugar, flour and salt.
3. Add the dry ingredients to the egg yolk mixture alternately with the milk, starting and ending with the flour, e.g., 1/3 of the flour, 1/2 of the milk, 1/3 of the flour, remaining milk, remaining flour.
4. In a separate clean bowl, with clean beaters, beat the egg whites until stiff peaks form. Then, on the slow speed of the mixer, beat the egg whites into the yolk mixture.
5. Pour the mixture into an ungreased 8" (20 cm) square baking pan. Set the baking dish in a pan of hot water so that the water comes up 1" (2.5 cm) around the dish.
6. Bake in a 350°F (180°C) oven for 45 minutes. The top should be golden brown and the center shouldn't jiggle.

Serves 6-9.

SERVING SUGGESTION: This is great whether served warm or cold. We add just a dollop of whipped cream and a fresh mint leaf to dress it up.

NOTE: This doubles very well for a 9 x 13" (23 x 33 cm) baking dish, but add 10 minutes to the baking time.

* *This is equal to the juice of 1 lemon.*

Boreal Bread Pudding
with Brandy Sauce

We know what you're thinking. "Why would anyone bother to put a bread pudding recipe in a modern cookbook?" We all tend to think of bread pudding as something Mom threw together when she didn't have anything really good on hand. But wait until you taste this.

12 cups	cubed day-old French bread	3 L
1½ cups	raisins	375 mL
6	eggs	6
6 cups	whole milk	1.5 L
1½ cups	white sugar	375 mL
2 tbsp.	vanilla extract	30 mL
2 tbsp.	brandy	30 mL

1. Spread the bread cubes in a greased 9 x 13" (23 x 33 cm) pan. Sprinkle with the raisins, distributing them evenly throughout.
2. Beat together the eggs, milk, sugar, vanilla and brandy with a wire whisk and pour over the bread cubes. Cover and refrigerate. You can leave it overnight if you like or put the pudding together early in the morning to bake that evening.
3. Set the pan in a larger pan of hot water and bake at 350°F (180°C) for 50-60 minutes. The pudding is done when it is set in the middle. It should act like set gelatin when you lightly shake the pan.
4. Prepare the Brandy Sauce, below, and serve it warm over the bread pudding.

Serves 15.

Brandy Sauce

½ cup	butter OR margarine	125 mL
2 cups	brown sugar	500 mL
2 cups	half and half (we use evaporated milk)	500 mL
¼ cup	brandy OR bourbon*	60 mL

1. Heat the butter and brown sugar over medium heat. Add the half and half, stirring constantly. (We use a wire whisk for this.) Heat until bubbly and slightly thickened. Add the brandy. Be careful as it will probably bubble up. Cook for about 30 seconds then remove from the heat.

SERVING SUGGESTION: Serve warm over the bread pudding.

* *You might want to start with 2 tbsp. (30 mL) of the brandy and then add a bit more to taste.*

Peach Cobbler with Spiced Cream

If you are fortunate enough to live where fresh peaches are available most of the year, this is a recipe for you. But we have made it with canned peaches, too, and we still end up passing out plenty of seconds!

Peach Layer:

1½ tbsp.	cornstarch	22 mL
⅓ cup	brown sugar	75 mL
½ cup	cold water	125 mL
4 cups	sliced, peeled peaches	1 L
1 tbsp.	butter OR margarine	15 mL
1 tbsp.	lemon juice	15 mL

Batter Topping:

¾ cup	flour	175 mL
¾ cup	sugar	175 mL
¾ tsp.	baking powder	3 mL
¼ tsp.	salt	1 mL
3 tbsp.	butter OR margarine at room temperature	45 mL
1	large egg, slightly beaten	1
1 tbsp.	milk	15 mL
1 tbsp.	white sugar	15 mL

1. Combine the cornstarch, brown sugar and water in a heavy pot. Add the sliced peaches and cook until thickened, about 5 minutes. Remove from the heat and add the butter and lemon juice.
2. Put the peach mixture into a round or square 8" (20 cm) baking pan. Set aside while you make the topping.
3. Combine the flour, sugar, baking powder and salt. Add the butter, egg and milk and mix until smooth.
4. Drop by spoonfuls over the hot peach mixture and sprinkle the top with the 1 tbsp. (15 mL) of white sugar.
5. Bake at 400°F (200°C) for 40-50 minutes, until the top is golden brown.

Serves 6.

Spiced Cream

1 cup	whipping cream	250 mL
2 tbsp.	liquid honey	30 mL
½ tsp.	cinnamon	2 mL

1. While the cobbler is baking, whip all ingredients until soft peaks form. If you have one of those whipped cream machines that use the CO_2 cartridge, you can use that. (Yes, even with liquid honey.)

NOTE: This recipe doubles well. Bake it in a 9 x 13" (23 x 33 cm) pan.

Chocolate Mousse Flan

This is much simpler than it looks — very simple but very impressive. We like our guests to think we spend hours on each dessert. This one can be made a day ahead or early in the morning to give it all day in the refrigerator.

1 cup	flour	250 mL
2 tbsp.	icing sugar	30 mL
1 oz.	square semisweet chocolate, melted	30 g
1/2 cup	butter OR margarine, at room temperature	125 mL
1/3 cup	whipping cream	75 mL
5 x 1 oz.	squares semisweet chocolate	5 x 30 g
2 tbsp.	butter OR margarine	30 mL
2	eggs, separated	2
1/4 cup	white sugar	60 mL
2 x 1 oz.	squares semisweet chocolate, coarsely grated	2 x 30 g

1. Combine the flour, sugar and 1 oz. (30 g) chocolate. Cream in the 1/2 cup (125 mL) butter until smooth and well mixed (like shortbread dough). Form the dough into a ball and press into the sides and bottom of a 9½" (24 cm) flan pan* with removable sides. Chill for 1 hour and then bake in a 425°F (220°C) oven for 10 minutes. Cool completely.
2. Bring the whipping cream to a boil and add the 5 squares of chocolate and the 2 tbsp. (30 mL) butter. Turn the heat to low and stir until all the chocolate is melted. Do not boil. Blend in the egg yolks well, stirring constantly. Remove from the heat. Allow to cool for 10 minutes.
3. While the chocolate mixture is cooling, beat the egg whites until frothy. Gradually add the sugar, beating until stiff peaks form. Fold into the chocolate mixture and pour into the pastry crust. Chill for 5 minutes.
4. Sprinkle grated chocolate over the mousse filling.

Serves 8.

SERVING SUGGESTION: Icing sugar sifted over the top, just before serving, adds a nice touch.

* *A flan pan is like a pie plate with 1½" (4 cm) high fluted edges and a bottom that lifts out.*

Mocha Marble Cheesecake

The first time Marie made this she didn't read the last instruction. "Cover and refrigerate overnight or for up to 2 days." Give yourself lots of time. It's worth it.

1 cup	chocolate wafer crumbs	250 mL
2 tbsp.	butter OR margarine, melted	30 mL
1 cup	semisweet chocolate chips	250 mL
8 oz.	cream cheese	250 g
¾ cup	sugar	175 mL
3	eggs	3
1 tbsp.	lemon juice	15 mL
2 tsp.	vanilla	10 mL
pinch	salt	pinch
3 cups	sour cream	750 mL
2 tsp.	instant coffee granules	10 mL
1 tbsp.	hot water	15 mL

1. To make the crust, stir together crumbs and melted butter until well moistened. With back of a spoon or your hands, press crumbs onto the bottom of a lightly greased springform pan. Bake in a 325°F (160°C) oven for 8-10 minutes, or until set. Let cool.
2. Center the springform pan on a square of foil; fold up the foil around the sides, to keep out the water when baking the cheesecake, later.
3. To prepare the cheesecake, melt the chocolate chips over low heat, stirring constantly until just melted. Set aside to cool.
4. In a large bowl, beat cheese until softened. Gradually beat in sugar for 3 minutes, or until smooth and light, scraping down bowl twice.
5. Using low speed, beat in eggs, one at a time, beating well after each addition and scraping down the bowl often. Blend in lemon juice, vanilla and salt. Blend in sour cream.
6. Dissolve coffee in 1 tbsp. (15 mL) hot water. Divide cheesecake batter in half. Whisk chocolate, then coffee, into one half.
7. By cupfuls (250 mL), alternately pour chocolate batter and plain batter over the crust. Swirl a knife through the batter, without disturbing the crust, to create a marbled effect throughout.
8. Set the foil covered springform pan in a larger pan. Pour enough water in the outer pan, 1" (2.5 cm) up the sides of the springform pan.
9. Bake at 325°F (160°C) for 1¼ hours, or until the shine disappears and the edge is set, yet the center still jiggles slightly.
10. Turn off oven. Run a knife around edge of cake. Cool cake in the oven for 1 hour. Remove from water; place on a rack; remove foil. Let cool.
11. Cover and refrigerate overnight or for up to 2 days.

Serves 16.

SERVING SUGGESTION: Using the Chocolate Topping for the Chocolate Cake Roll, page 167, spread or drizzle some chocolate sauce on the plate before adding the slice of cheesecake. Garnish with a fresh strawberry.

Desserts

Blueberry Cream Cheese Tart

This is what it is all about — this is why Marie and Helen are sometimes nowhere to be found. They are out picking blueberries so they can bring you this tantalizing tart! We like to use wild blueberries because the flavor is superior. If you use commercial berries, use the smaller berries.

Crust:

½ cup	butter OR margarine	125 mL
¼ cup	sugar	60 mL
1 cup	flour	250 mL
¼ tsp.	grated dried orange rind OR 1 tsp. (5 mL) fresh	1 mL
½ tsp.	vanilla	2 mL

Cream Cheese Lemon Filling:

8 oz.	cream cheese, at room temperature	250 g
½ cup	sour cream	125 mL
½ tsp.	grated dried lemon rind OR 1 tsp. (5 mL) fresh	2 mL
¼ tsp.	nutmeg	1 mL
¼ cup	white sugar	60 mL

Blueberry Topping:

½ cup	fresh blueberries*	125 mL
¼ cup	sugar	60 mL
2½ cups	fresh OR frozen blueberries	625 mL

1. To prepare the crust, cream butter and sugar. Add remaining ingredients and cream well. Press into the bottom and sides of a 9" (23 cm) pie pan.
2. Bake the crust in a preheated 375°F (190°C) oven for 15-20 minutes. It should be a nice golden brown.
3. Remove from the oven and let cool on a rack until completely cooled.
4. To prepare the filling, cream the cream cheese well and then beat in the remaining ingredients until smooth.
5. Spread the filling in the cooled pie shell.
6. To make the topping, combine the ½ cup (125 mL) of blueberries and sugar in a saucepan over medium heat. Simmer for 5 minutes, then remove from the heat. Add the remaining blueberries. Cool completely, then spread over the cream cheese filling.
7. Refrigerate for at least 4 hours to blend the flavors.

Serves 8-10.

SERVING SUGGESTION: Serve this very showy dessert on a glass plate with a dollop of whipped cream and a few fresh blueberries on the side.

* *If you are using frozen berries, add 2 tbsp. (30 mL) of cornstarch, dissolved in 3 tbsp. (45 mL) of cold water, to the blueberry and sugar mixture for the last minute of cooking. Then just remove from the heat and add the rest of the berries.*

Pie Pastry

(HELEN) Let's talk about pastry! From my experience with my three daughters and the women who have worked with me at the lodges, pastry is one of the most intimidating challenges they face. Marie and I don't use the same recipes for our pastry. Hers is slightly saltier and mine is slightly sweeter. They are both nonfail and they bring rave reviews whether we use them for our main course pies or desserts. We have shared these recipes with sisters, children and friends and they all have moved from the "I can't make pastry" class to "Hey, this is easy!"

These make enough for 3, 2-crust pies. If you don't need it all, just roll the dough into 1-crust-sized balls, store them in a freezer bag and either refrigerate or freeze depending on how long it will be before you use them. Bring the dough to room temperature before rolling it out.

Helen's Pastry

5 cups	flour	1.25 L
1 tsp.	baking powder	5 mL
1 tsp.	salt	5 mL
1 lb.	lard	500 g
1	egg	1
1 tbsp.	vinegar	15 mL
1 tsp.	brown sugar	5 mL
	cold water	

1. Mix together the flour, baking powder and salt.
2. Cut in the lard with a pastry blender until the mixture is crumbly and the lard is distributed like little peas throughout the flour.
3. Break the egg into a measuring cup; beat with a fork and add the vinegar and brown sugar. Beat again and add water to the 1-cup (250 mL) mark. Pour the water mixture around the edge of the flour mixture while stirring with a fork. Be sure to moisten all the flour but do not overmix. Divide the dough into 6 equal balls. (1 ball equals 1 pie crust.)
4. Sprinkle a board or counter top liberally with flour and roll out dough with a floured rolling pin, adding more flour if necessary. Place the dough in a pie plate, add filling and cover with the top crust. Cut vents to allow the the steam to escape.

Makes pastry for 3 double-crust pies or 6 single-crust pies.

Cinnamon Pastry Rolls

Never throw away leftover pastry! Make Cinnamon Pastry Rolls. Roll out any amount of pastry in a rectangular shape. Spread with butter, sprinkle liberally with brown sugar and cinnamon. Roll up, starting from a long side. Cut into 1" (2.5 cm) slices and put on an ungreased baking pan. Bake at 450°F (230°C) for 10 minutes, or until slightly browned.

Desserts

Marie's Pastry

5½ cups	flour	1.375 L
2 tsp.	salt	10 mL
1 lb.	lard	500 g
1	egg	1
2 tbsp.	vinegar	30 mL
	cold water	

Just follow the steps for Helen's Pastry, omitting the baking powder and sugar. Don't worry about overmixing this one. Part of its claim to fame is that it can be rolled and rerolled and not get tough!

Fruit Pie Fillings

Use your favorite fruit or custard fillings or one of the following fillings.

Apple Pie

7 cups	sliced, pared apples	1.75 L
1 cup	white sugar	250 mL
2 tsp.	cinnamon	10 mL
1 tbsp.	butter	15 mL

Combine the first 3 ingredients and spread in a prepared, unbaked, pastry shell. Dot with butter. Cover with top crust and cut vents for the steam to escape. Bake at 450°F (230°C) for 15 minutes. Reduce heat to 350°F (180°C) for 50-55 minutes longer.

Blueberry or Saskatoon Pie

4½ cups	fresh berries	1.125 L
¼ cup	flour	60 mL
¾ cup	white sugar	175 mL
2 tbsp.	butter	30 mL

Combine the first 3 ingredients and spread in prepared, unbaked, pastry shell. Dot with butter. Cover with top crust and cut vents for the steam to escape. Bake at 450°F (230°C) for 15 minutes. Reduce heat to 350°F (180°C) for 50-55 minutes longer, until filling is thickened and bubbles up through the slits and around the edges.

NOTE: Fruit pies tend to boil over; place a pan under them to catch the drips.

VARIATION: When using frozen berries, use 1 extra cup (250 mL) of white sugar. Substitute an equal amount of cornstarch for flour. Cook 5 minutes longer at high heat and cook 10 minutes longer at 350°F (180°C).

Puff Pastry

This can be used in any dessert or savory recipe calling for puff pastry.

2 cups	flour	500 mL
½ cup+2 tbsp.	water	150 mL
2 tsp.	oil	10 mL
1 tbsp.	vinegar	15 mL
½ tsp.	salt	2 mL
½ cup+2 tbsp.	cold butter	150 mL
⅓ cup	flour	75 mL

1. In a bowl, combine 2 cups (500 mL) flour, water, oil, vinegar and salt to make a dough.
2. Place on a floured surface and knead until smooth and shiny. If you have a kitchen machine with a dough hook, use it for this step.
3. Wrap the dough with plastic wrap and refrigerate for 1 hour.
4. Cut the butter into pieces into a bowl, add the ⅓ cup (75 mL) flour and work until well combined. (The dough hook works well here too.) On a floured surface, shape the butter into an 8" (20 cm) square. Place on waxed paper and refrigerate.
5. Place the dough on a well-floured surface and roll into an 8 x 16" (20 x 40 cm) rectangle. Place the butter square on ½ of the dough and fold the other ½ over. Press the edges of the dough together firmly to completely seal in the butter.
6. Now roll the dough to a little less than ¼" (1 cm) thickness. Fold ⅓ of the dough into the centre, brush off the flour from the top and fold the other ⅓ on top of the first. (There should now be 3 layers of dough.) This is a single fold.
7. Now roll the dough in the opposite direction. Fold both edges to meet at the centre, brush off the flour and fold over again to make 4 layers, a double fold.
8. Wrap the dough rectangle in plastic and refrigerate for 1 hour.
9. Remove the dough from the refrigerator and roll out for 1 more single and 1 more double fold. Wrap in plastic again and refrigerate for at least 1 more hour.
10. The dough is now ready to use. It keeps for days in the refrigerator or can be frozen.

Makes about 2 lbs. (900 g) of Puff Pastry.

Fruit Turnovers

Roll out Puff Pastry dough and cut into 6" (15 cm) squares. Put 2 tbsp. (30 mL) of your favorite fruit pie filling in the middle of each square. Brush edges with beaten egg. Fold squares corner to corner to form a triangle. Press to seal edges. Brush with beaten egg; cut a slit in the top. Sprinkle with sugar and place on an ungreased baking sheet. Bake at 375°F (190°C) for 15-20 minutes.

Irresistible Pecan Pie

If you are a pecan pie lover as I am you will enjoy this one. You will find that it is not overly sticky sweet, so give it a try. Use one of the pastry recipes found on pages 184 and 185, or your own favorite.

½ cup	butter OR regular (not light) margarine, melted	125 mL
½ cup	sugar	125 mL
1 cup	golden corn syrup	250 mL
½ tsp.	salt	2 mL
1 tbsp.	vanilla	15 mL
3 tbsp.	flour	45 mL
3	eggs	3
2 cups	coarsely chopped pecans	500 mL
1	unbaked 9" (23 cm) pie shell with a high rim	1

1. Pour the melted butter into a mixing bowl. Add the sugar, syrup, salt, vanilla, flour and eggs and beat well. Fold in the pecans.
2. Pour the filling into the pie shell. Bake at 425°F (220°C) for 10 minutes, then lower the temperature to 350°F (180°C) and continue baking for about 40 minutes. Test the pie by shaking gently. If the centre is like set gelatin it is done. Cool to room temperature before slicing.

Serves 8-10.

SERVING SUGGESTION: I prefer this after it has been chilled, with a nice dollop of whipped cream or ice cream.

Bless each of our families
Bless this food that we eat
May we be a blessing
To all that we meet.
Christian Renewal Centre, Oregon

Bavarian Apple Torte

(HELEN) This fantastic dessert came from an Australian friend who was a nurse in Churchill for a number of years. It's a big hit with our guests.

¼ cup	sugar	60 mL
½ cup	melted butter OR margarine	125 mL
1 cup	flour	250 mL
½ tsp.	vanilla	2 mL
8 oz.	cream cheese, at room temperature	250 g
⅓ cup	sugar	75 mL
1	egg	1
1 tsp.	vanilla	5 mL
4 cups	thinly sliced peeled apples	1 L
½ cup	sugar	125 mL
1½ tsp.	cinnamon	7 mL
⅓ cup	ground OR slivered almonds	75 mL

1. Mix together the sugar, melted butter, flour and vanilla. Press into the bottom and sides of a 9" (23 cm) pie plate. Set aside.
2. Beat together the cream cheese, sugar, egg and vanilla until smooth. Pour into the lined pie plate.
3. Mix together the apples, sugar and cinnamon and spoon carefully over the cream cheese mixture. Sprinkle with the almonds.
4. Bake at 350°F (180°C) for 45-55 minutes, or until the apples test tender and the crust is golden brown.

Serves 8.

SERVING SUGGESTION: Add a dollop of whipped cream to each serving.

NOTE: We like to make this the day before we serve it. The flavors are much stronger when it has been allowed to sit in the refrigerator overnight.

The Johnny Appleseed Grace

The Lord is good to me
And so I thank the Lord
For giving me the things I need
The sun and the rain and the appleseed
The Lord is good to me.

And every seed I sow
Will grow and grow and grow
And some day there'll be apples there
For everyone in the world to share
The Lord is good to me
Johnny Appleseed — Amen

  *Desserts*

Pavlova Nests from "Up Over"

(HELEN) This is a northern adaptation of a very southern dessert. It is delicious. The traditional way to make Pavlova is in one large nest but we found that it is much easier to serve if we make little individual nests.

Meringue Nests:

4	egg whites	4
¼ tsp.	cream of tartar	1 mL
⅛ tsp.	salt	0.5 mL
1 cup	white sugar	250 mL

1. Combine egg whites, cream of tartar and salt. Beat until frothy. Add the sugar 1 tbsp. (15 mL) at a time, beating well after each addition. Beat until stiff glossy peaks form.
2. Spread baker's or waxed paper on 2 large, greased cookie sheets. Using 2 spoons, make 12 meringue nests about 3" (7 cm) in diameter. Form nests slightly higher on the sides with a bit of a dip in the middle.
3. Bake at 300°F (150°C) for 40 minutes, or until very delicately colored around the edges. Turn off the oven and leave nests to cool in the closed oven. These can be made several days ahead and stored in a cardboard box. Do not refrigerate.

Lemon Filling

3 tbsp.	cornstarch	45 mL
¾ cup	sugar	175 mL
¼ tsp.	salt	1 mL
¾ cup	boiling water	175 mL
2	egg yolks, beaten	2
1 tbsp.	butter	15 mL
½ tsp.	grated dried lemon peel OR 1 tsp. (5 mL) fresh	2 mL
¼ cup	lemon juice	60 mL

1. Combine cornstarch, sugar and salt in a heavy saucepan. Gradually add the boiling water. Cook, stirring constantly, until thick and clear.
2. Stir about ½ cup (125 mL) of the hot mixture into the egg yolks, stirring constantly. Stir this back into the hot mixture, return to low heat and cook, still stirring, for 2-3 minutes.
3. Remove from heat and stir in the butter, lemon peel and juice. Cool.

Serves 12.

SERVING SUGGESTION: Place a Pavlova Nest on each plate. Fill with lemon filling, a dollop of whipped cream and top with fresh fruit. (We use wild blueberries, bananas, strawberries, kiwi, melon.) Try passion fruit if available.

See photograph on page 173.

Fruit Pizza

This very showy dessert is sure to impress. Make it in a 9" (23 cm), 10" (25 cm) or 11" (28 cm) flan pan with removable sides and cut it at the table.

Almond Crust:

¼ cup	ground almonds	60 mL
½ cup	butter OR margarine	125 mL
½ cup	white sugar	125 mL
1½ cups	flour	375 mL
1	large egg yolk	1
1 tsp.	vanilla	5 mL
1 tsp.	almond extract	5 mL

Apricot Glaze:

½ cup	apricot jam	125 mL
1 tbsp.	butter	15 mL
1 tbsp.	lemon juice	15 mL
2 tbsp.	Amaretto OR Apricot Brandy	30 mL

Amaretto Filling:

8 oz.	cream cheese, at room temperature	250 g
3 tbsp.	white sugar	45 mL
2 tbsp.	amaretto OR apricot brandy	30 mL
1 tsp.	vanilla	5 mL
½ tsp.	almond extract	2 mL
	assorted fruits (see step #5)	

1. To prepare the crust, cream the almonds, butter, sugar, flour, egg yolk and extracts together until the dough sticks together very well.
2. Press dough on bottom and ½" (1.3 cm) up sides of pan. Bake at 375°F (190°C) for 15 minutes, until lightly browned. Set aside to cool.
3. Stir glaze ingredients together in a small pot over medium heat until the jam is melted; stir well. Set aside to cool.
4. To prepare the filling, beat the cheese with the sugar, amaretto, vanilla and almond extract until light and fluffy. Spread over the cooled crust.
5. Arrange fruit in a pleasing pattern to cover the surface of the pizza. We use combinations of strawberries, kiwi, grapes, bananas, oranges, nectarines and plums. Choose fruit with a nice combination of colors in mind and arrange it in a circular pattern starting at the outside edge.
6. With a pastry brush, brush the cooled glaze over the fruit, covering the entire surface. Refrigerate until ready to serve.

Serves 8-12.

Desserts

Strawberry Temptation Puffs, page 193
Strawberry Orange Sauce, page 194

Strawberry Temptation Puffs

We think the name says it all for this dessert. This is our own invention and it has quickly become a regular on the menu.

Cream Puffs or Profiteroles:

1 cup	water	250 mL
1/4 tsp.	salt	1 mL
1/2 cup	butter OR regular margarine	125 mL
1 cup	flour	250 mL
4	eggs	4

1. To make the cream puffs, put the water, salt and butter into a heavy saucepan. Bring to a boil and add the flour all at once. Stir vigorously with a wooden spoon until the dough leaves the side of the pan and forms a smooth ball. Remove from the heat and let cool for 2 minutes.
2. Add the eggs, 1 at a time, beating well after each addition. Be sure the egg has been completely absorbed into the batter and that the batter is smooth and glossy before adding the next egg. (If you have a kitchen machine with a dough hook, it can be used for this step).
3. Drop the dough by heaping tablespoonfuls (30 mL) onto a greased cookie sheet. Make 12 puffs of equal size.
4. Bake at 400°F (200°C) for 10 minutes. Turn the oven temperature down to 350°F (180°C) and continue to bake for 30-40 minutes. It is better to bake the puffs a little longer to guarantee that they won't collapse when taken from the oven.
5. Remove the puffs from the oven; prick them on the bottom to allow the steam to escape. Cool puffs on a wire rack while you make the filling.

Strawberry Filling

1/2 cup	whipping cream	125 mL
2 tbsp.	sugar	30 mL
8 oz.	cream cheese, at room temperature	250 g
1 tbsp.	cream OR evaporated milk	15 mL
3/4 cup	sliced fresh strawberries	175 mL

1. Whip cream and sugar until soft peaks form and it holds its shape.
2. In a separate bowl, with an electric mixer, beat the cream cheese and 1 tbsp. (15 mL) cream. Add the whipped cream and beat until fluffy.
3. Refrigerate the filling until just before serving. At serving time, fold in the sliced strawberries.

Aurora Borealis –

The Northern Lights at Dymond Lake Lodge
(Photo by Dennis Fast.)

Strawberry Orange Sauce

¼ cup	sugar	60 mL
¼ cup	water	60 mL
1 cup	puréed fresh OR frozen strawberries	250 mL
1 tsp.	grated fresh orange rind OR ½ tsp. (2 mL) dried	5 mL
2 tsp.	frozen orange juice concentrate	10 mL
¼ tsp.	lemon juice	1 mL

1. In a small saucepan, bring the sugar and water to a boil and simmer for 5 minutes. Cool slightly and add the strawberries, orange rind, orange concentrate and lemon juice. Refrigerate until serving time.

TO ASSEMBLE:
1. Add the sliced strawberries to the cream filling.
2. Put a small amount of sauce on individual serving plates and swirl it to cover the centre portion of the plates.
3. Cut the tops off of the puffs and fill the puffs with cream filling. Replace tops and set puffs on plates.
4. Drizzle a bit of sauce over the top of each puff.
5. Garnish each plate with 2 whole strawberries on the side of the puff.

Serves 12.

See photograph on page 191.

Be present at our table, Lord
Be here and everywhere adored
Thy creatures bless, and grant that we
May feast in Paradise with Thee.
John Cennick (1718 — 1755)

Sauces, Jams, Jellies & Juices

A northern cookbook wouldn't be complete without us telling you what we do with all the extra berries we pick on a good year. We've also thrown in some other favorites that we make at home and serve at the camps.

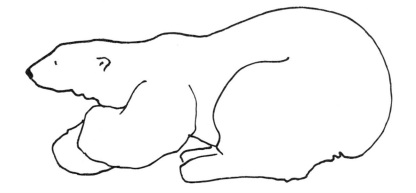

Sterilizing Jars

The best jars to use are Mason jars which are made of heavier glass, specifically for home canning. You can purchase replacement inserts for the lids, and so guarantee a good seal no matter how many times you use the jars. We also use any glass jar that comes with a lid that has a rubber seal on the interior. Avoid lids that have cardboard inserts.

The recommended method for sterilizing jars is to place them in a canner (if you have one) or a large pot and cover them with water. Bring water to a boil and boil 10 minutes at altitudes up to 1,000 ft. Boil 15 minutes at altitudes of 1,001-3,000 ft. Lids need only be boiled for 5 minutes.

Heating jars in the oven is not recommended. Breakage can occur when jars are being filled with hot liquids. This could have serious consequences.

I have to confess that we aren't very careful in this area. We usually settle for pouring boiling water over the jars. This is OK if the preserve is going to be eaten fairly quickly and stored in a refrigerator; or if the preserve has been boiled for more than 10 minutes. But to ensure safe results, properly sterilize all jars used in recipes which require less than 10 minutes processing time. Processing time for most fruit, pickles and tomatoes is 10 minutes or longer.

The Chilly Awakening

(DOUG AND HELEN WEBBER, GARY AND MARIE WOOLSEY) The first day of the canoe trip had been challenging. We had tipped one canoe, lost one boot and a fishing pole, and numerous things were soaked. But our spirits were high. We pitched the tent and cooked dinner before the rain started. One sleeping bag was too wet to use, so with two double air mattresses side by side, one bag as a bottom sheet and one bag per couple as blankets, we arranged ourselves with women to the inside, and fell asleep to the patter of rain on the roof and the rush of the river outside .

Sometime later, I (Helen) awoke feeling intensely cold. The sleeping bag had slipped down between the mattresses and was eagerly slurping up the rivulet running through our tent on its way to the river. My posterior was taking a dip in that rivulet. Gives a whole new meaning to the title, A River Runs Through It, doesn't it?

The river sounded a whole lot closer. It was, in fact, little more than a metre from our door. But the rain had slowed, and our concern was to dry things out. We had no dry or warm footgear, and the thrill of the trip had been somewhat dampened. Cold feet tend to do that! But in true pioneer spirit, as the men got fires going and clothing smoking, the women started up the one-burner element and cooked bacon, eggs and, the pièce de résistance, Camping Bannock — all inside the tent. Never has breakfast tasted better. The pleasure of that breakfast was surpassed only when the men arrived bearing dry and WARM rubber boots! Heavenly!

Sauces, Jams, Jellies & Juices

Mustard Dill Sauce

We use this sauce with Stuffed Baked Lake Trout, page 32, Crispy Fried Fish, page 28, and Mike's Beer Batter Fish, page 30.

1 cup	mayonnaise OR salad dressing	250 mL
¼ cup	prepared mustard	60 mL
1 tsp.	dried dillweed	5 mL

1. Combine all ingredients and serve. Store leftover sauce in the refrigerator.

Makes 1¼ cups (300 mL) of sauce.

Honey Dill Sauce

A delicious dip with anything you deep-fry.

1½ cups	mayonnaise	375 mL
1 cup	liquid honey	250 mL
2 tsp.	dried dillweed	10 mL

1. Combine all ingredients and serve. Store leftover sauce in the refrigerator.

Makes 2½ cups (625 mL) of sauce.

Provençale Sauce

Great with Stuffed Baked Lake Trout, page 32, or steamed vegetables.

½ cup	butter	125 mL
1 tbsp.	Provençale*	15 mL

1. Melt butter and add Provençale. Mix well and serve.

Makes ½ cup (125 mL) of sauce.

* *See the note on Provençale on page 34.*

Grand Marnier Sauce

Serve this luscious sauce as a special treat over French toast, pancakes or waffles. Crêpe Suzette flavor with a fraction of the work.

1½ cups	maple syrup	375 mL
1 cup	butter OR margarine	250 mL
1½ tsp.	grated orange rind	7 mL
2 tbsp.	Grand Marnier	30 mL

1. In a small saucepan, combine all ingredients and heat until butter is melted.

Makes about 2½ cups (625 mL) of sauce.

Cranberry Sauce

This is probably the easiest sauce you will ever make. We serve it almost exclusively with goose and turkey, but we have had guests who like it on their toast!

4 cups	cranberries	1 L
2 cups	white sugar	500 mL
1 cup	water	250 mL

1. Combine all ingredients in a medium-sized saucepan. Bring to a boil and simmer for 10 minutes, or until berries have popped and the sauce has begun to thicken. Store in jars in the refrigerator.
2. For longer storage, sterilize* jars and seal while hot.

Makes 6 cups (1.5 L) of sauce.

* *See note on STERILIZING JARS on page 196.*

Blueberry Sauce

This sauce is great served hot over pancakes or waffles, or cold over ice cream.

2 cups	blueberries, fresh OR frozen	500 mL
½ cup	white sugar	125 mL
2 tbsp.	butter OR margarine	30 mL
¼ tsp.	nutmeg	1 mL
1 tbsp.	lemon juice	15 mL

1. In a saucepan, mix blueberries, sugar, butter and nutmeg. Bring to a boil and simmer for 5 minutes. Add lemon juice.
2. Store remaining sauce in the refrigerator.

Makes 2 cups (500 mL).

See photograph on page 51.

Sauces, Jams, Jellies & Juices

Fruit Sauce

Serve with Wild Meatball Taste Teasers, page 8, or Chicken Fingers.

3 tbsp.	cider vinegar	45 mL
1 cup	apricot OR peach jam	250 mL
1/4 tsp.	paprika	1 ml

1. Mix well and serve.

Makes about 1 1/4 cups (300 mL) of sauce.

Black Currant Sauce

Serve with roast pork or caribou.

1 1/2 cups	black currant jam	375 mL
2 tbsp.	corn syrup	30 mL
1/4 cup	red wine vinegar	60 mL
1/4 tsp.	salt	1 mL
1/2 tsp.	cinnamon	2 mL
1/2 tsp.	nutmeg	2 mL
1/2 tsp.	cloves	2 mL
1/2 cup	slivered almonds	125 mL

1. Combine all of the sauce ingredients, except the almonds, in a heavy saucepan over medium heat. Heat to boiling, reduce the heat and simmer for 2 minutes. Remove from the heat and add the almonds. Keep the sauce warm until serving time.

Makes about 2 1/4 cups (550 mL) of sauce.

Black Currant Jam

We have a patch of black currants at Dymond Lake that is so loaded with berries that we feel duty bound to relieve the poor bushes of their load.

4 cups	black currant pulp*	1 L
4 cups	sugar	1 L

1. In a heavy, medium-sized saucepan, combine pulp and sugar, and bring to a boil, stirring frequently.
2. Boil for 15-20 minutes, or until the jam thickens a little, stirring to prevent scorching.
3. Pour the jam into hot, sterilized** jars and seal. Allow to cool.

Makes about 6 cups (1.5 L) of jam.

* *Unless you are a very clean picker, you will have to remove the berries from their stems. Press the berries through a sieve to remove the skins.*
** *See note on STERILIZING JARS on page 196.*

Elma's Rhubarb Jam

Rhubarb is a hardy plant that does indeed grow in the far north, though not wild. One year, when Elma was working with us in the kitchen, she made some rhubarb jam that the staff dubbed "Elma's jam", and it was in great demand. We hope you'll like it too. We use fresh rhubarb and frozen strawberries.

5 cups	rhubarb	1.25 L
1 cup	thawed frozen strawberries	250 mL
5 cups	white sugar	1.25 L
3 oz.	pkg. pineapple gelatin	85 g

1. Chop the rhubarb into bite-sized pieces.
2. In a large heavy saucepan, combine rhubarb, strawberries and sugar with a little water. Bring to a boil and boil for 15 minutes, or until rhubarb softens and starts to break up.
3. Add the gelatin powder and stir well, until thoroughly dissolved.
4. Pour the jam into hot, sterilized* jars and seal immediately. Allow to cool.

Makes 9 cups (2.25 L) of jam.

* *See note on STERILIZING JARS on page 196.*

Ripe Gooseberry Jam

Gooseberries contain an abundance of natural pectin and flavor. When ripe, they make a wonderfully rich-tasting jam. The only drawback is that they are fairly scarce, and painful to pick — thorns, you know! So we guard our supply rather jealously.

4	parts gooseberry pulp (see Step. #1)	4
2-3	parts sugar	2-3
1	part water	1

1. Ripe gooseberries are purple or red. Wait until they have attained that colour before picking them. Put the gooseberries through a sieve to remove the stems and skins, but get as much pulp as possible.
2. Measure the pulp. Add half that amount of sugar and one quarter that amount of water. This gives a fairly tart jam. If you like a sweeter jam, increase the sugar to 3 parts.
3. Boil over low heat, stirring frequently, for 15-20 minutes, or until the jam thickens a little.
4. Pour the jam into hot, sterilized* jars and seal. Allow to cool.

* *See note on STERILIZING JARS on page 196.*

Sauces, Jams, Jellies & Juices

Doug's Peach Honey

We call this Doug's Peach Honey because Doug, in a rare moment of culinary creativity, was the first one to make it. We all loved it so much that we called for an encore — alas, too late — the moment had passed. So now we make it ourselves.

12	large peaches	12
1	large orange	1
	white sugar	

1. Drop the peaches into boiling water. Leave them for 1-2 minutes. Remove peaches and slip off their skins. Remove the pits.
2. Put the seeded orange, including peel, and the peaches through a food chopper or blender.
3. Measure the fruit mixture and add an equal volume of sugar in a large heavy saucepan.
4. Bring to a boil and simmer until the jam reaches the desired consistency, approximately 20 minutes.
5. Pour the jam into hot, sterilized* jars and seal immediately. Allow to cool.

Makes about 10 cups (2.5 L) of jam.

* *See note on STERILIZING JARS on page 196.*

Raspberry Jelly

This is one common berry that we can't get our hands on in our area of the north. So, as an alternative to fresh raspberry jam, we're including a jelly made from frozen raspberry juice. Great flavor!

2 cups	frozen raspberry concentrate	500 mL
2 cups	sugar	500 mL
1 cup	water	250 mL
6 oz.	bottle liquid Certo, OR 2 pouches	170 mL

1. In a medium-sized heavy saucepan, bring juice, sugar and water to a boil. Add the Certo. Boil for 4 minutes, pour the jelly into hot, sterilized* jars and seal immediately. Allow to cool.

Makes 4 cups (1 L) of jelly.

* *See note on STERILIZING JARS on page 196.*

Crab Apple Jelly

For the last 10 years, Marie has lived in places where there are good supplies of crab apples. A lot of her jelly makes its way to the camps. She makes it without adding pectin, which gives less jelly, but a very nice flavor.

6 cups	crab apple juice (see below)	1.5 L
2 tbsp.	lemon juice	30 mL
6 cups	white sugar	1.5 L

1. To prepare the juice, wash the crab apples. Do not peel or core them. Place them in a large pot, filling the pot about ⅔ full. Add water to just barely cover them. Boil the crab apples until the skins have split and the colour has gone into the liquid, about 15 minutes.
2. Put the apples through a sieve, pressing them very gently so that only the liquid goes through, not the pulp. (If you wish to make applesauce, sieve the pulp into another container. Later on, you can heat it gently and add sugar to taste.)
3. Strain the crab apple liquid through cheesecloth. This will remove any pulp and give a clear jelly. Measure 6 cups (1.5 L) of juice.
4. To make jelly, in a medium-sized heavy saucepan, boil the crab apple juice with lemon juice and sugar until the liquid is reduced, and the juice starts to gel when tested on a metal spoon. This could take 30 minutes or more.
5. Pour the jelly into hot, sterilized* jars and seal. Allow to cool.

Makes about 7 cups (1.75 L) of jelly.

* *See note on STERILIZING JARS on page 196.*

Crab Apple Juice

Crab apples make a wonderful pink-colored apple juice. If you have an abundant supply, this is a very practical and delicious way to use them.

4 qts.	crab apples, halved OR quartered	4 L
1 tbsp.	cream of tartar	15 mL
5 qts.	boiling water	5 L
	sugar to taste	

1. Place the prepared apples, cream of tartar and boiling water in a very large container. I use a plastic dishpan. Cover and let sit for 30 HOURS.
2. Strain out the apples. Measure the juice.
3. Boil the juice with ¼ cup (60 mL) sugar per quart (L) of juice. Taste and add more sugar if desired.
4. Pour the juice into hot, sterilized* bottles and store in a cool place.

Makes about 6 quarts (6 L) of juice.

* *See note on STERILIZING JARS on page 196.*

Index

SHARE WITH A FRIEND

$4.00 (TOTAL ORDER) FOR SHIPPING AND HANDLING

Blueberries & Polar Bears _____ x $21.95 = $_____

Cranberries & Canada Geese _____ x $19.95 = $_____

Black Currants & Caribou _____ x $19.95 = $_____

Icebergs & Belugas (comprehensive index) _____ x $21.95 = $_____

Wild & Wonderful – Blueberries _____ x $5.95 = $_____

Wild & Wonderful – Cranberries _____ x $5.95 = $_____

Wild & Wonderful – Fish _____ x $5.95 = $_____

Wild & Wonderful – Goose & Game _____ x $5.95 = $_____

Wild & Wonderful – Wild Rice _____ x $5.95 = $_____

Postage and handling (total order) _____ = $___$4.00___

Subtotal _____ = $_____

In Canada add 7% GST _____(Subtotal x .07) = $_____

Book Total _____ = $_____

DLS – 4 oz. (113 g), see page 3 _____ x $4.00 = $_____

DLS – 12 oz. (340 g), see page 3 _____ x $9.00 = $_____

Total enclosed _____ = $_____

U.S and international orders payable in U.S. funds./Price is subject to change.

Name: _____

Street: _____

City: _____ Prov./State: _____

Country: _____ Postal Code/ZIP: _____

Please make cheque or money order payable to:

Blueberries & Polar Bears Publishing
Box 6104 Calgary South P.O.   OR   P.O. Box 304
Calgary, Alberta   Churchill, Manitoba
Canada T2H 2L4   Canada R0B 0E0
Fax/Phone: (403) 251-9569/1-800-490-2228
E-mail: mwoolsey@bbpbcookbooks.com

For volume purchases, contact
Blueberries & Polar Bears Publishing for volume rates.
Please allow 2-3 weeks for delivery.

www.bbpbcookbooks.com

BLUEBERRIES & POLAR BEARS – The FIRST batch of our most requested recipes. Recipes for Moose, Goose and Things that Swim introduce this comprehensive collection of outrageously good recipes for breakfasts, lunches and dinners. Splendid food photos are backed up with northern landscape photos.

CRANBERRIES & CANADA GEESE – The SECOND batch of our most requested recipes. Imaginative wild game and fish recipes, plus a new array of tempting recipes for appetizers to desserts, developed for easy preparation, using good basic ingredients. Superb on-site food and northern landscape photos.

BLACK CURRANTS & CARIBOU – The THIRD batch of our most requested recipes. The glorious scenery and superb hunting and fishing at Webber's Lodges are surpassed only by the array of succulent breakfast, lunch and dinner dishes. The splendid food and landscape photos were shot on site at Dymond Lake Lodge north of Churchill.

ICEBERGS & BELUGAS – The FOURTH batch of our most requested recipes. Pristine northern wilderness and the Belugas and icebergs of Hudson Bay are the setting and inspiration for this extraordinary collection of delicious recipes enjoyed by the fortunate guests at Webber's Lodges. Stunning on-site photos.

The above books are 7" x 10", 208 pages, 18-24 colour photos, lay-flat coil binding.

WILD & WONDERFUL:

BLUEBERRIES
CRANBERRIES
FISH
GOOSE & GAME
WILD RICE

The *Wild & Wonderful* books provide the best possible range of Cranberry, Blueberry, Fish, Goose & Game, and Wild Rice recipes in small affordable books designed for easy preparation, using good basic ingredients. Ideal for gift giving or your personal pleasure, *Goose & Game* and *Fish* recipes include appetizers, soups, roasts, stews, sausages and more. *Blueberries* and *Cranberries* recipes include muffins, loaves, cookies, brownies, cheesecakes, pies, jellies, vinegars and making your own dried berries. *Wild Rice* recipes include baking, appetizers, soups, salads, side and main dishes, even desserts.

The above books are 5¼" x 8¼", 48 pages, saddle stitched binding.